OVERVIEW

Overview

Some people argue that workplaces are conducive to rapid growth and development of conflict. What's your opinion?

A study by Watson and Hoffman revealed that 42 percent of a manager's time is spent on reaching agreement with others when conflicts occur in the workplace.

Conflict management is a demanding part of a manager's duties, and most managers no doubt think that they could spend this time more productively.

But this does not mean that conflict is always negative. In fact, there are several ways to view conflict in the workplace.

People usually perceive conflict in one of three ways. Maurice, Joanne, and Abbie - for example - each view conflict differently. Joanne believes that conflict is a good thing, while Maurice believes it is a bad thing. Abbie takes the view that conflict can present opportunities for positive change.

See each employee to learn more about their view of conflict.

Maurice

Maurice believes that conflict is a bad thing. In his view, conflict is always destructive. It inevitably creates many problems between workers, and so should be eradicated from the workplace.

Joanne

Joanne thinks that conflict creates challenge, and that through challenge and adversity the natural leaders in any workplace situation will be identified. To her, conflict enables the strong to survive at the expense of the weak.

Abbie

Abbie believes that conflict can be both good and bad. She feels that too much conflict is a negative force, but that some conflict is stimulating and energizing, because arguments make people justify and rethink their points of view.

Abbie's view represents the approach that this course will take--that a degree of conflict should be encouraged as a way to stimulate ideas and promote change.

This course will show you how to encourage conflict in the workplace that will result in more creativity, more energy, and more ideas.

Once you have developed a good understanding of conflict, you can:
- encourage healthy differences between workers,
- recognize conflict in the workplace when it occurs.

This course will help you to identify the signs and symptoms of destructive conflict, so that you can more easily recognize when conflict will negatively impact upon employees.

You will also see the benefits that can be gained from encouraging healthy differences between people. You will discover how to manage conflict in the workplace in a way that fosters positive outcomes.

CHAPTER ONE

Perspectives on Conflict in the Workplace

Views of Conflict

Conflict in the workplace is not a one-dimensional phenomenon. There are many interpretations of its effects on organizations.

According to Wilson and Rosenfeld, part of a manager's salary is "combat pay" for dealing with the aggravation that conflict in the workplace brings. Many people share this view.

The language that these people use to describe conflict says a lot about their real feelings. They think that conflict is negative, and so use images that emphasize this aspect.

Some people view conflict as always being a bad thing in organizations, but others hold the opposite view--that conflict is always a positive influence in the workplace.

This view is based on the idea that conflict is the natural human condition, and that everyone is dominated by survival instincts. The strong survive, but the weak do not, and so conflict is one of the most effective ways to sort the weak from the strong. This approach is often referred to as Social Darwinism, after Charles Darwin's writings about the way that species evolved on Earth.

Other people take the view that conflict isn't necessarily good or bad. Instead, they stay in the middle ground, believing that conflict can be managed to produce positive outcomes.

This view is sometimes called the interactionist perspective, and is the generally accepted current view of conflict in the workplace.

Constructive conflict in the workplace

Conflict in the workplace is not a one-dimensional phenomenon. There are many interpretations of its effects on organizations.

Consider the situation at the Marmaris Hotel, where Jenny is a new reception clerk. Conrad is her co-worker, and Abel works in the hotel restaurant.

Jenny: I was worried that some guests were waiting a long time to settle their accounts. The duty receptionist didn't agree with me at first, but I showed him that one guest had to wait ten minutes--and now my manager understands. It's so much better than my last place, where we argued all of the time, without any productive results.

Jenny says in a concerned tone.

Conrad: You must have picked the right place and time. Everybody needs a bit of a challenge now and then.

I think that you were right--we have gotten lazy about check outs.

Conrad says in a friendly tone.

Abel: In the restaurant, we used to spend so much time arguing about the dining room layout that one time we were late preparing it for lunch. Our manager soon got us back on track, although we're still debating the perfect arrangement. We really try to appreciate each other's points of view.

Abel says in a neutral tone.

Jenny and her colleagues show that conflict in an organization can potentially be either constructive or destructive. It is destructive when it goes too far, or is conducted at the wrong time and place.

It is constructive when it is used as a means for improvement, and is controlled and managed with this end in mind.

In other words, conflict needs to be appropriate in scale, purpose, and context.

Learning how to manage conflict so that it is constructive brings many benefits. Constructive conflict:

- enhances performance by challenging complacency;
- improves group cohesiveness;
- facilitates organizational change.

Question

Jed has always avoided conflict, because he thinks that it inevitably leads to destructive feelings within the organization. But Karen thinks that conflict can be constructive. What are the benefits of constructive conflict that Karen might highlight to Jed?

Options:

Managing Workplace Conflicts

1. Conflict in the workplace can improve memory retention. 2. Conflict can make a working group more cohesive.
3. Conflict can challenge complacency in the workplace.
4. People can use conflict to gain promotion.
5. Conflict can facilitate change in the workplace.

Answer:

Constructive conflict in the workplace can lead to more cohesive groups, and by facilitating positive change, it will challenge complacency.

Option 1: This choice is not correct. There is no known connection between workplace conflict and memory retention. The improvement of memory retention is influenced by factors unrelated to conflict in the workplace.

Option 2: This choice is correct. If conflict is managed well, it can improve group cohesion because it challenges people to work together to resolve conflict.

Option 3: This is a correct choice. Employees can become complacent if there is too much agreement. Conflict can be an energizing force in an organization and can result in increased productivity.

Option 4: This is not a correct choice. Conflict in the workplace is not necessarily a way to gain career advancement. Conflict can often lead to a stymied career path.

Option 5: This option is correct. If conflict is managed well, it can foster organizational change by encouraging people to consider diverse points of view.

A healthy organization fosters constructive conflict. Challenging complacency in the correct context promotes change and cohesiveness, which ultimately leads to growth.

A negative view of conflict

According to Wilson and Rosenfeld, part of a manager's salary is "combat pay" for dealing with the aggravation that conflict in the workplace brings. Many people share this view.

The language that these people use to describe conflict says a lot about their real feelings. They think that conflict is negative, and so use images that emphasize this aspect.

People with this negative view do not see conflict as productive. They often use extreme language to talk about it, describing conflict as:
- destructive, by using words such as warfare, battles, and casualties,
- uncontrolled or irrational, by talking about rage, or saying that someone has "lost control",
- violent, by highlighting the pain, suffering, and wounds experienced by those involved in it.

Question

Jack hates conflict in the workplace because he sees it as a negative force. Based on this information, select the statements that are likely to be Jack's.

Options:

1. "We quarreled about the methods, but that resulted in a quicker way in the end."

2. "I've seen colleagues fighting just to make somebody else look stupid in front of the boss."

3. "Bill lost his bonus because he argued so much with Amy."

4. "We had an informed debate on the new proposals about ethics."

5. "People use vicious tactics here to get their way."

Answer:

Jack has a negative view of conflict, and so he will describe it in terms of destruction, fighting, wounding, and irrationality.

Option 1: This option is incorrect. This is not likely to be Jack's statement because it presents conflict in a positive light. The conflict resulted in a better solution.

Option 2: This is a correct choice. This sounds like a statement Jack would make about conflict. It reveals a negative view of conflict in that people are using it to criticize and belittle others in front of superiors.

Option 3: This choice is correct. This is likely to be Jack's statement because this statement shows a cause-and-effect relationship between conflict and something bad happening to a coworker.

Option 4: This is not likely to be one of Jack's statements because it doesn't reflect a negative view of conflict. It seems to imply that the debate on the new proposals was a worthwhile activity.

Option 5: This is likely to be Jack's statement because it borrows from warfare terminology to frame conflict in a negative light.

People who hold a negative view of conflict interpret even minor disputes as dysfunctional. Chuck, one example, takes this approach.

I hate team meetings, as people are always arguing. Even the simplest decision takes forever, and often we don't even make one unless I exercise my authority. At the last meeting, somebody suggested changing our regular venue. But nothing else would be dealt with if I let the discussion get started, so I vetoed it.

In fact, I'm against teamwork. As far as I can see, it just creates anxiety. Put a team together to do a job, and somebody always ends up unhappy. It's a fight for power and control between the team members, and the losers just opt out.

Then the next time you want the losers to work with someone else, they don't want to. They want to work on their own. Their ideas have been dismissed so many times that they are not even willing to talk about them. It's their way, or nothing.

See each characteristic in turn for a fuller description.

Time-wasting

When conflict is viewed negatively, it is seen to be inefficient. Time spent having an argument is really a devious way to avoid work. In this view, the notion that arguing helps people get rid of strong feelings and energy implies that time has been wasted because it could have been much better spent doing actual work.

Detrimental effect on people

In this negative view, conflict is seen to cause stress. If people can't say anything without having to justify it, then they're often tense and fearful of each other. Chuck says that teamwork just doesn't work when everything is debated.

A "bunker" mentality

In Chuck's view, people are being forced to avoid challenges, and so have become reluctant to discuss their opinions. They are closing up, operating in a defensive mode because they feel like they are being attacked.

Question

Managing Workplace Conflicts

Jackie works with various colleagues who have negative views of conflict. Match the beginning of each statement from Jackie's colleagues with an end so as to correctly categorize the different aspects of this negative view.

Options:

A. "I think that conflict produces a bunker mentality because it

B. "Conflict always has a detrimental effect on people, because it

C. "Conflict is another name for time-wasting, because it

Targets:

1. causes stress."
2. is inefficient."
3. makes people feel like they're being attacked, so they close down."
4. makes teamwork impossible."
5. is just a reason for avoiding work."

Answer:

In this view, conflict is seen as harmful to people because it causes stress and prevents teamwork, creates a bunker mentality by making people close down, is an inefficient use of time, and lets people avoid work.

"Conflict always has a detrimental effect on people, because it causes stress." In this negative view, conflict is seen to cause tension and discomfort.

"Conflict is another name for time-wasting, because it is inefficient." People who hold this negative view see no benefits to conflict. They simply think it is a waste of precious time.

"I think that conflict produces a bunker mentality, because it makes people feel like they're being attacked so they close down." People who view conflict in this way believe that people operate in a defensive mode when conflict arises.

"Conflict always has a detrimental effect on people, because it makes teamwork impossible." This negative perspective views conflict as a barrier to effective collaboration.

"Conflict is another name for time-wasting, because it is just a reason for avoiding work." In this negative view, time spent having an argument is really a work-avoidance strategy.

The traditional view of conflict in many organizations is that it is bad, and that it must be avoided and suppressed because it is unproductive. Companies also fear the effect that conflict will have on relationships between employees.

But when this negative view takes hold, employees fear conflict so much that they end up in either "fight" or "flight" mode, attacking or running away. They are primed to be overly defensive, which makes them incapable of working together efficiently.

A positive view of workplace conflict

Some people view conflict as always being a bad thing in organizations, but others hold the opposite view--that conflict is always a positive influence in the workplace.

This view is based on the idea that conflict is the natural human condition, and that everyone is dominated by survival instincts. The strong survive, but the weak do not, and so conflict is one of the most effective ways to sort the weak from the strong. This approach is often referred to as Social Darwinism, after Charles Darwin's writings about the way that species evolved on Earth.

In his book "The Gamesman" Michael Maccoby describes two personality types found in modern organizations which typify this "survival of the fittest" approach.

See each personality type to learn more.

The jungle fighter

This person experiences work as a jungle, where the mantra is "eat or be eaten." Winners destroy losers. The reward is survival, while others perish.

The gamesman

For this person, the game is everything. The gamesman competes not for the rewards, but just for the sake of competing, and winning.

Question

Ben works in a small team, and each of the team members has a different view of conflict. Statements from Ben's colleagues are listed. Which ones typify a positive view of conflict?

Options:

1. "Conflict can help us to resolve our differences amicably."

2. "Conflict is just part of the human condition. It's natural."

3. "We're all dominated by our survival instincts. Conflict is just a way of getting rid of the losers."

4. "Conflict is good because it helps us to work together well."

5. "Conflict helps us to get rid of those who can't deal with pressure. People who can cope are better able to do their jobs."

Answer:

In fact, the positive view is based on the idea that conflict is natural, and that everyone is struggling against each other to survive. Conflict is seen as a necessary way to remove the less able or weak.

Option 1: This statement does not typify a positive view of conflict because it implies that differences can be worked out without negative feelings. In fact, conflict may result in an outcome that is unacceptable to some.

Option 2: This statement is positive because it views conflict as a natural occurrence that can actually help strengthen an organization.

Option 3: This is a correct statement. This perspective is based on the idea that the strong survive but the weak do not, and so conflict is one of the most effective ways to sort the strong from the weak.

Option 4: This statement does not typify a positive view of conflict because it conveys the notion that conflict leads to effective collaboration. In fact, conflict creates a competitive work environment.

Option 5: This option is correct. This view is based on the idea that conflict can help you get rid of low performers, which will lead to increased competence in the workplace.

When this positive view of conflict is applied to the business setting, it results in certain attitudes and propositions.

These are that:
- conflict encourages strong employees to prevail over weak ones,
- managers must pay close attention to a naturally lazy workforce,

- conflict demands competition between people, not collaboration.

But many people would characterize these proposals as extreme, and counter them by pointing out that good ideas can be suppressed under this sort of regime. Constructive compromises and the benefits of pooled ideas will not be encouraged in such a competitive atmosphere. Employees who are less assertive, but who have a valuable contribution to make, will be intimidated by the aggressors.

Consider the case of Ntel Corporation. The Board has taken its motto from General George S. Patton's words: "In case of doubt, attack." Ntel Corporation prides itself on being an organization that is determined to be successful, no matter what.

See each statement to learn what Xtel's chief executive has to say about the company's work ethic.

Statement 1

"We believe in the survival of the fittest. In our organization, everything is up for grabs. The strongest get the rewards. That way, we only employ winners."

Statement 2

"You can't put people together without them challenging each other. It's not natural. We're all in competition with each other. Nobody wants to be a loser."

Statement 3

"We expect our managers to be in control. We know that our employees want to get away with doing as little as possible, and we expect our managers to be driving them to work harder the whole time."

Statement 4

"If an idea is any good, it needs to be tested against every possible argument. If you put an idea forward here, then you have to destroy all challengers. Otherwise it isn't worth considering."

This view of conflict supports individualism and competition. Leaders lead and the workforce has to follow. There is little or no concern about the effect of the conflict on the losers. Rewards are reserved for the winners only.

Question

Charles is being interviewed for a position at Ntel Corporation. The interviewer asks him what he thinks about conflict in the workplace. Charles believes that conflict is vital at work, for three main reasons. Which statements is Charles likely to use?

Options:

1. "An idea is worth nothing if you can't defend it against all attackers."

2. "Conflict in my team was all about compromise."

3. "I've always been the best, and I expect my staff to fight to show me that they are also the best."

4. "People tend to be lazy, but I won't have that. I know how to make people work hard – all the time." 5. "If co-workers disagree with my ideas, it helps us to create a better solution."

Answer:

As someone who feels that all conflict is positive, Charles's comments will reflect the idea that competition produces winners, that the staff needs constant supervision, and that competition is better than collaboration.

Option 1: Charles is likely to use a statement such as this. This statement reflects the view that if an idea is worth considering, it must be tested. When ideas are put to the test, only the most valuable ones survive.

Option 2: Charles is not likely to use this statement about conflict because it reflects the idea that conflict supports collaboration and less effective outcomes.

Option 3: This is a statement that Charles would make. It reflects his belief that conflict promotes competition, which enhances workplace performance.

Option 4: Charles is likely to use a statement such as this to express his belief that conflict is a strategy supervisors can use to get the most out of their employees.

Option 5: This is not a statement Charles is likely to make because it reflects the belief that conflict leads to collaboration. Charles believes that conflict fosters competition.

A positive view of conflict is based on the belief that, through struggle and competition, the strongest survive. In the workplace, strong employees win by defeating weaker ones, managers rigidly rule their staff, and there are no abstract ideas, only people to be fought.

But this fails to recognize the benefits of synergy and compromise. Most people would like to work for an organization where they are valued, rather than where they have to fight for survival. Wouldn't you?

Conflict can be managed

Some people take the view that conflict isn't necessarily good or bad. Instead, they stay in the middle ground, believing that conflict can be managed to produce positive outcomes.

This view is sometimes called the interactionist perspective, and is the generally accepted current view of conflict in the workplace.

The interactionist perspective is based on the assumption that too much conflict is a bad thing, but an organization needs a certain level of conflict to function effectively. This is because conflict:
- is neither inherently good nor bad
- is inevitable in organizations
- can be beneficial for all, rather than just the winners.

Conflict can be viewed on a continuum, from being a positive influence in an organization to a negative influence. Therefore, there can be an optimum level of conflict, so long as it is managed effectively.

Managers who follow the interactionist perspective do not blame people for expressing their differences in healthy and constructive ways. In fact, they will try to encourage these differences.

This encouragement is based on a belief about the true nature of conflict in the workplace. The interactionist perspective argues firstly that conflict cannot be avoided, and secondly that it is neither inherently good nor inherently bad.

See each aspect of the interactionist view to learn more about it.

Conflict cannot be avoided

Human nature dictates that people will have differences of opinion. This will always happen. Differences can be suppressed, but they will still exist. If conflict is inevitable, it is better to harness it than suppress it, and so conflict needs to be managed.

Conflict is neither good nor bad

The value of conflict is not fixed, but depends on the circumstances in which it happens. In different contexts, the same form of conflict could have a beneficial or adverse effect. It depends on how it is managed.

The notion of encouraging some conflict in the workplace contradicts the view that conflict is a bad thing.

When managers aim for an optimum level of conflict, they need to be very clear about the benefits that it will bring.

See each benefit of conflict to learn more about each one.

Allows processing of emotion

The processing of emotion is essential for human well-being. Healthy conflict allows this, whereas hidden grudges give rise to irrational acts. Through healthily expressed conflict, people's true feelings are exposed.

Helps group development

Conflict helps group development by enabling discussion about roles and norms. Individuals in the group who might have been reluctant to disagree can be encouraged to participate more.

Enhances creativity

Creativity is enhanced when people must justify their ideas, hear other points of view, and rethink their propositions. The results of such challenges can be synergistic. Challenge also exposes previously unrecognized issues.

Consider how conflict is managed in Brad and Sonya's team meeting. They are debating how to handle a new account.

Brad: I know it feels as though I'm always disagreeing with you, but are you actually suggesting that we make Tony the account manager?
Brad says in a slightly incredulous tone.
Sonya: I hope you will disagree if you have a valid point--that's the way it should be. But I still think that Tony's the best candidate. What have you got against him? It's still not that business with the Menzies account, is it? I proved that it wasn't his fault.
Sonya says getting defensive.
Brad: OK, I admit that it was still in my mind. But even so, I don't think that Tony has the financial background to be credible with stockbrokers. Do you?
Brad says in a pleasant tone.
Sonya: I hadn't thought of that angle. But he's got all of the other credentials--more than the other candidates. Look, I still really think that he's the right one for this job.
Sonya says in a thoughtful tone.
Brad: OK! OK! I'll agree if that's how you feel. What we need to do then, is give him support from someone with more financial experience.
Brad says in a slightly annoyed tone.
Sonya: Sure. I'll do that.
Sonya says in a pleased tone.
Sonya and Brad shared their opposing points of view and solved the problem. This is because their conflict made them more creative, and improved their relationship. Both of them realize that they can benefit from conflict, if they treat each other sensitively.

In his book on organizational behavior, Stephen Robbins describes a real life example of the interactionist perspective. At ME International, the president challenged his workers to develop a statement of corporate values.

See each action performed at ME International to learn how healthy differences were generated in the organization.

President hired a consultant

The president hired a consultant to facilitate and maintain an ongoing level of conflict during the process.

Employees were encouraged to express personal beliefs

The consultant encouraged employees to express personal beliefs, and to openly question and disagree with others' ideas.

Question

Of the examples given, what statements could the president of ME International use to justify the interactionist perspective?

Options:

1. "Conflict can be a beneficial process for the entire workforce, not just the aggressive people."

2. "There is no optimum level of conflict in an organization. It's just necessary."

3. "Conflict is not an absolutely good force in an organization, nor absolutely bad."

4. "Conflict is inevitable, so you need to work out how to manage it well."

5. "You can't manage conflict--it's just always there."

Answer:

Actually, the interactionist perspective sets out the view that there is an optimum level of conflict, if it is managed effectively. Conflict is inevitable, but neither inherently good nor bad.

Option 1: This is a comment the president could use to justify the interactionist perspective. Companies can benefit from conflict because it helps establish good relationships, functional groups, and creativity.

Option 2: The president would not use this statement to justify the interactionist perspective because it acknowledges that too much conflict is a bad thing. It holds that there is an optimum level of conflict; it just needs to be managed effectively.

Option 3: This is a statement that the president of ME International could use to justify the interactionist perspective. It reflects the notion that conflict is neither inherently good nor inherently bad.

Option 4: This is not a statement that justifies the interactionist perspective. Although this perspective argues that conflict is inevitable, it also maintains that conflict must be managed.

Option 5: This is a comment that the president could make; it reflects the interactionist perspective that conflict cannot be avoided. The thinking is that differences of opinion are inevitable with groups of people.

Conflict, at the right level, is a healthy and energizing force in an organization. But it must be managed carefully to ensure that it works creatively, and not destructively.

Encouraging Healthy Differences

One of the most effective ways to manage conflict in the workplace is to accept its inevitability, and use it positively. This approach could be described as encouraging healthy differences.

How could you start to encourage healthy differences in your workplace? One answer is to stimulate sensible competition among employees.

Healthy differences create sensible competition that energizes without distracting from productivity. Healthy competition challenges the mentality that is satisfied with "good enough."

Democracy is one of the greatest forces for good in Western society. An integral part of this democratic tradition is debate, which is formalized argument and challenge.

When you think about conflict in the workplace, as in sport, the usual assumption is that if there is a winner, then there must also be a loser.

But you can reconfigure conflict situations in a way that makes everyone involved a winner.

Benefits of encouraging healthy differences

One of the most effective ways to manage conflict in the workplace is to accept its inevitability, and use it positively. This approach could be described as encouraging healthy differences.

John has to make a presentation tomorrow to his company's management committee, outlining the attitude that it should take towards conflict, and the reasons for that approach.

But after attending a conference called "Conflict in the Workplace" he has become confused. It appears that there are some quite different--and even opposing--views of conflict.

John, for example, recalls three memorable presentations at the conference. The speakers all had very different views of conflict.

Connie: We are afraid of the consequences of conflict, and so our approach is to suppress it. This means that the workforce is rarely challenged. Unfortunately, this ignores, and in some cases condones poor performance. Bad practices are common, and the workforce is expected to be obedient.

Says Connie

Ivan: Here, conflict is the dominant operating style. It pervades our relationships, and workers are in competition with each other. For us, there can only be one winner, and so the majority of staff have stopped trying. Winners and losers are polarized.

Says Ivan

Natalie: We encourage "healthy differences." Enough conflict has energized employees, and made them more competitive and challenging of each other. But here, competition is not personal. It is for the good of the company.

Says Natalie

After reviewing his notes, John starts to come around to the view that encouraging healthy differences is probably best for his company.

He begins his presentation to the committee by identifying the benefits of encouraging healthy differences.

See each of John's four points to review extracts from his presentation.

Point 1

"Our staff will really benefit from productive arguments. We've missed them lately--we've all been too careful not to upset each other, and haven't come up with our best ideas. We can definitely be more imaginative this way."

Point 2

"I think we've become lazy. The last time I asked for comments on a new procedure, nobody replied. It didn't turn out well, and I'm sure that a couple of guys expected that. But they didn't speak up. I want my people to challenge me."

Point 3

"What's wrong with celebrating success? Julie won a big contract, and no one noticed. She needed the praise, and others needed to see her getting it. If they had, they'd be after some of it, as well. I want my team to try to be the best."

Point 4

"Of course, encouraging healthy differences won't be easy. Anybody who thinks that it's a quick fix is wrong. It'll take time and effort to see the benefits in terms of a happier and more productive workforce. But it will pay dividends in the end."

Some people argue that conflict in organizations is always unproductive, because it distracts employees from their work.

But John's conclusion is that even if healthy differences will cause some disruption to productivity in the short-term, the longer-term gains in terms of creativity, challenge, and competition are worth it.

Question

Harry, Marsha, Kyle, and Betty have come to different conclusions about the benefits of healthy differences in their organizations. Three of them recognize that there

are benefits, but one of them is not sure. What three views identify the benefits of healthy differences?
Options:
1. "We'll be able to stimulate creativity."
2. "It will immediately increase productivity."
3. "It will challenge complacency."
4. "For us, it will foster energizing competition."

Answer:
Encouraging healthy differences will positively impact upon creativity, challenge, and competition. Short-term productivity may be disrupted, although this will reverse in the long-term.

Option 1: This comment identifies one of the benefits. Healthy differences can produce productive arguments and stimulate innovation. Effective arguments are energizing and make parties consider and justify their positions.

Option 2: This statement is not correct. Healthy differences will not necessarily result in an immediate boost in productivity. Although differences may enhance productivity, it will happen over a longer period of time.

Option 3: This comment identifies one of the benefits of healthy differences. On occasion, people within organizations become complacent and unproductive. Healthy differences can stimulate productivity.

Option 4: This statement reflects one of the benefits of healthy differences. Healthy differences create sensible competition that energizes without distracting from productivity.

If you can encourage healthy differences in your team, then the gains can be transformational. Over time, you will see creativity increase, productive competition flourish, and complacency disappear.

Stimulating healthy competition

How could you start to encourage healthy differences in your workplace? One answer is to stimulate sensible competition among employees.

Healthy differences create sensible competition that energizes without distracting from productivity. Healthy competition challenges the mentality that is satisfied with "good enough."

See each company to learn how its employees experienced competition in the workplace.

Farr Incorporated

"John Farr threw me out of a meeting for disagreeing with him. He is still totally in charge. If you want a promotion, you have to show him that you're better than your boss. If he could make us fight a duel, he would."

Candle Time

"I like working at Candle Time, in quality assurance. We might send as much stuff back as we pass, but the arguments are fun. Look at Annie's new design. It took some debating, but the final version we came to was better than her original."

The Lazy Steer Company

"The Lazy Steer is a nice family business. Mom runs it now that Dad has passed on, and she knows what works. My sister Sondra wants to advertise on the Internet, but Mom isn't going to upset the advertising agency that we've always used."

Unlike the other two companies, Candle Time has found a middle ground between too much competition, and too little competition.

It has promoted healthy competition by:
- making opportunities available to everyone,
- distributing rewards evenly,
- using objective performance measures.

Question

Jerome is meeting with Japanese counterparts in his firm. He recognizes that the prevailing culture in the Japanese branch of the company is not as competitive as in the North American branch. What advice should he give to Japanese colleagues about promoting healthy competition?

Options:

1. He should tell them to encourage bending of the rules.
2. He should advise them to apply objective performance measures. 3. He should point out that opportunities must be available to all.
4. He should indicate that they must distribute rewards evenly.

Answer:

Actually, Jerome needs to advocate objective performance measures, a fair reward system, and equal opportunities. These all encourage healthy competition. Cheating is counter-productive, and will only encourage resentment.

Option 1: Jerome's telling his Japanese counterparts to bend the rules does not encourage healthy competition. Bending the rules encourages cheating, which fosters a negative and unjust work environment.

Option 2: This option is correct. Jerome should recommend that his Japanese colleagues use objective criteria to define success. That way, everyone can be measured against the criteria, and all who meet those criteria will succeed.

Option 3: This option is correct. To help his Japanese colleagues promote healthy competition, Jerome should tell them to make opportunities available to everyone. Such opportunities include the chance to be promoted or implement new ideas.

Option 4: This is correct. Jerome should advise his Japanese counterparts to challenge employees by rewarding attempts at competition. For those who do not succeed, the recognition may encourage them to make more effort next time.

A common analogy is made between competition in organizations, and competition in sports. Through competition, new records are constantly being set.

But sports are governed by rules that enable competition to be positive, and not destructive. In sports, those who cheat are penalized, and play must be fair, so that everyone can have a chance to excel.

At Candle Time, competition works. But John Farr's aggression dominates his company, and The Lazy Steer Company lives up to its name. Mom is complacent. So, how has Candle Time stimulated healthy competition?

Organizations like Candle Time have not just developed healthy competition in the workforce by chance. They have identified and implemented some specific ways of behaving that will stimulate the right sort of competition.

See each of the three factors for encouraging healthy competition to learn more about it.

Opportunities

Opportunities are open to everyone. The chance to be promoted, to bid for work, or to implement ideas is not restricted to a favored few. Challenges can come from anywhere and anyone in the organization, and opportunities are not limited to only a few staff members.

Rewards

Rewards are not just for winners. By rewarding entry to the competition, more people are encouraged to challenge themselves and others. For those who do not succeed, the recognition may encourage them to make more effort next time.

Performance criteria

Use objective criteria to define success. Reputation and status should not be significant. Objective criteria need to be fair and transparent. That way, everyone can be measured against the criteria, and all who meet those criteria will succeed.

Question

You are responsible for trying to promote healthy competition in your organization. You have prepared a presentation that highlights the key changes required. Unfortunately, you dropped your slides, and they are now out of order. Match the beginning of each sentence with the correct ending so that the slides correctly describe the actions required to promote healthy competition.

Options:

A. Opportunities are
B. Rewards are
C. Performance measures are

Targets:
1. not limited to only a few staff, but are available to all.
2. fair and transparent.
3. not just for the winners, but for all those who try.

Answer:
For healthy competition, opportunities must be open to all, rewards must not just be for winners, and your performance criteria must be fair and transparent.

Opportunities are not limited to a few employees; they are available to all. The opportunity to be promoted, to bid for work, or to implement ideas is not restricted to a select few but available to everyone.

Performance measures are fair and transparent. When objective criteria are used to define success, everyone can be measured against the criteria, and all who meet those criteria will succeed.

Rewards are not just for winners; they are for all those who try. By rewarding entry to the competition, more people are encouraged to challenge themselves and others.

Candle Time, for example, has a series of posters to encourage healthy competition among workers. They show the staff why the company values this approach so much.

Actions like the ones implemented at Candle Time are not difficult to introduce. One of the easiest ways to start is at the team level. How would you turn a team that ineffectively uses the competitive spirit into one that embodies healthy competition?

Now apply your knowledge about how you stimulate healthy competition in a different situation.

Keep these three points in mind as you resolve the problems at Kiddiworld:
- Make opportunities available to everyone.
- Distribute rewards evenly.
- Use objective performance measures.

Case Study: Question 1 of 3

Scenario

You are Kiddiworld's president, and sales are falling. You think that part of the reason is the way that competition is approached in the company. When you first started, Kiddiworld was very competitive. You changed that for a more cooperative approach.

Now you feel that it has gone too far, and people have become complacent. So you want to reintroduce a bit more competition, but at a productive level.

Encourage healthy competition in Kiddiworld by answering the questions that follow, in order.

Question

One area of concern is the way that staff members are approaching training. In the old days, people got support for training by shouting the loudest, but lately they seem to be expecting you to nominate who should take courses. You want to bring healthy competition back into this area. What should you do?

Options:

1. I would hold a lottery for training places, as staff members would be energized by this novel approach.

2. I would advertise the courses to everyone. The only restriction on application would be job relevance.

3. I would give people a training allowance, and let them spend it how they liked.

4. I would make staff members pay for their own training. That way, only the keenest would do it.

Answer:

Healthy competition is open competition. This way, you have clearly made the opportunity available to anyone with an appropriate job. A lottery may involve people winning irrelevant places, and payment will prevent some from participating.

Option 1: This option is incorrect. A lottery is a random selection process that won't necessarily foster healthy competition. This approach may encourage passivity because selection is made by the luck of the draw.

Option 2: This choice is correct. Advertising the courses to everyone promotes healthy competition. This approach gives everyone who is qualified the chance to compete for training opportunities.

Option 3: This is an incorrect choice. Giving people a training allowance will not necessarily open the competition to everyone with an appropriate job.

Option 4: This option is incorrect. Requiring staff members to pay their own way will prevent those people who can't afford it from participating. This approach doesn't make this opportunity open to everyone.

Case Study: Question 2 of 3

Kiddiworld has a "Salesperson of the Month" bonus scheme. The idea is that all of the salespeople can apply for the bonus, and the winner takes the lot. How could you alter this system to encourage more healthy competition?

Options:

1. Increase the bonus, so that the stakes are raised.

2. Allocate the bonus on a rotating system, so that everyone gets a bonus over time.

3. Withdraw the bonus system completely, and incorporate the money into everyone's salaries.

4. Allocate points for every sale, and reward all staff members according to the number of points that they gain.

Answer:

Healthy competition will be encouraged by spreading the rewards more evenly. Rewards still need to be based on trying, though, and not be automatic, otherwise there will be no effort made.

Option 1: This choice is incorrect. Simply increasing the bonus does not address the problem that the current bonus scheme does not reward trying; it rewards winning. To promote healthy competition, you must base a reward system on trying.

Option 2: This is incorrect. Although a rotating bonus system is a fair one, it would not necessarily encourage healthy competition. Instead, it might encourage complacency because it is automatic and not based on performance.

Option 3: This is an incorrect option. Getting rid of the bonus system and incorporating the money into everyone's salaries is fair, but will not necessarily encourage more healthy competition. This is a solution that does not reward competition.

Option 4: This choice is correct. Allocating points for every sale and rewarding all staff members according to the number of points they have encourages healthy competition. It is a reward system based on trying, not on winning.

Case Study: Question 3 of 3

Promotion at Kiddiworld is based on an application, and a secret ballot among senior managers. How could you change this to encourage healthy competition?

Options:

1. Each manager should have to say who they supported.

2. The in-house magazine will publish the criteria for selection, which will be based on interviews, without the ballot.

3. An external recruitment agency should work under the direction of senior managers.

4. Unsuccessful candidates and their managers will jointly review why they did not get the promotion, based on the published criteria.

Answer:

Actually, healthy competition is encouraged when people can see clearly what the criteria for success are. The criteria also need to be objective and performance-based.

Option 1: This choice is not correct because it does not change the current process, which is pretty much a popularity contest. This process does not encourage healthy competition; it encourages favoritism.

Option 2: This is correct because this system uses objective criteria that are fair and transparent to define success. With this system in place, everyone can be measured against the criteria, and all who meet those criteria will succeed.

Option 3: This is incorrect because this approach does not inform the employees at Kiddiworld of the criteria that will be used for promotional purposes. Promotions may still be based on reputation and status rather than objective criteria.

Option 4: This option is correct. It allows candidates who don't receive promotions to clearly understand why they didn't. This supports a fair, competitive work environment.

As the Kiddiworld example shows, encouraging competition can be difficult because you're trying to achieve several different things at the same time.

By opening up opportunities, and making the criteria for success visible, you can reward more staff members. Then staff members don't have to fight to succeed.

Encouraging effective argument and challenge

Democracy is one of the greatest forces for good in Western society. An integral part of this democratic tradition is debate, which is formalized argument and challenge.

Ray and Jenny are talking about the way that challenge works in their organizations. Review the nature of the arguments that they use.

Ray: Where I work, people disagree with each other out of habit. Nobody will ever give in, or try to see the other person's point of view, so what we have are serial arguments. People take the opposite side from each other without thinking about it, and then defend and attack with vigor. And so on we go.

Says Ray in a mildly frustrated tone.

Jenny: Our place is like a boiler waiting to explode. On the surface it seems calm and reasonable, but really, everybody hates each other. Nobody says what they think, but everybody knows what everyone else's views really are. I can't stand it, so I just stay quiet.

Says Jenny in a frustrated tone.

Democracy is based on the notion that when people argue, they learn from each other. Arguing your case and being challenged to justify your opinion is a positive force in business, as much as in any other part of life.

Of course, too much can mean argument for argument's sake. But not enough can result in the failure to express feelings, which often leads to a sudden overreaction.

Effective arguments are energizing, and make both parties think, rethink, and justify their positions.

But if an argument is to be effective, then it needs to follow certain rules to ensure that it is rational. See each of the rules to learn more about it.

Arguments must be justifiable

Effective arguments need to be justifiable. This means using facts which can be verified, and not subjective opinions. "Cigarettes cause cancer" is a fact-based argument. "John Wayne was a good actor" is just opinion.

Arguments need to be on the same terms

One person might argue that oranges are the best fruit, but your favorite vegetable might be peas. This argument will never be effective, because each person is arguing about something different. To be effective, an argument needs to be on the same terms.

People don't have to agree

Sometimes people cannot, or do not, agree with each other. This does not mean that the argument is ineffective. Good arguments can end with both sides agreeing to differ, and accepting and honoring their differences.

Arguments are still effective even when people get angry with each other. Sometimes it seems easier to back off when the other side gets very emotional, but don't forget that, in the words of Horace: "Anger is a brief madness."

Lauren heard Jenny and Ray talking about their experiences of arguments. Now she describes a very different approach to them.

Lauren: I never really thought about it until I heard you guys describing your workplaces, but in my firm we really argue a lot with each other. So I suppose we're more like Ray's place, without the negativity.

Lauren says in a thoughtful tone.

Ray: What do you mean?

Ray says, sounding interested.

Lauren: Well, we argue and challenge each other passionately. But we walk away friends. I suppose that it's that old cliche about arguing with the idea, not the person. We're good at arguing, and we enjoy it.

Lauren says, in a friendly tone.

Jenny: How can you enjoy arguing with people?

Jenny says, sounding surprised.

Lauren: Yesterday, I disagreed with my team about lunch breaks. I end up answering the phones three times a week. That's not fair, and I showed them the schedule for the last six weeks to prove my point. Rick tried to argue that the holiday allocation evens it out, but we agreed that is a different argument.

Lauren says in an explanatory tone.

Ray: So what happened?

Ray says, sounding interested.

Lauren: In the end, we couldn't agree on a new permanent pattern. But that was OK--we aired our grievances. So I've produced a schedule for next month, and Rick will for the following month, and then we'll see which works best.

Lauren says in a matter of fact tone.

Lauren is clearly describing how debate can allow people to express their thoughts and feelings and help individuals to move forward from a disagreement. Lauren's experience highlights the fact that, although people won't always agree with each other, if arguments are based on facts and equal terms, then the outcomes can be positive.

Even if the best result of an argument is to "agree to disagree," this is preferable to frustrations boiling over, and relationships becoming strained.

Question

Greg doesn't agree with Kirsty's decision about budgets. When Greg tries to talk to her about it, she refuses to discuss it, saying that arguments are a waste of time. Greg tells Kirsty that if arguments are conducted properly, then they aren't a waste of time. How could Greg open his discussion with Kirsty to ensure that their discussion is effective?

Options:

1. "We don't have to agree with each other, but we do have to respect each other's point of view."

2. "I'm going to get the numbers to compare last month's spending with this month. Then we will have something concrete to work on."

3. "Let's not get too involved with the detailed numbers. That's too time-consuming."

4. "Let's start off by agreeing together that the issue is the entertainment budget. OK?"

5. "Your approach is completely irrational."

Answer:

Greg should focus on the facts of the situation, which in this case are the numbers. He should also be prepared to "agree to disagree" with Kirsty, and make sure that the argument is conducted on the basis of agreed terms.

Option 1: This option is correct. By acknowledging that they may agree to disagree, Greg is helping to ensure that their argument is rational. An argument can conclude with both sides agreeing to differ and accepting and honoring their differences.

Option 2: Correct. By using budget figures, Greg is ensuring that their argument is justifiable--based on facts that can be verified.

Option 3: This option is incorrect. If they don't take numbers into account, they will not have a sound basis for their argument. Greg and Kirsty should take the numbers into account as they proceed.

Option 4: Correct. Greg helps ensure the effectiveness of their argument by making sure it is on the same terms. He is clarifying that their argument is focused on the entertainment budget.

Option 5: This is not a correct choice. If Greg were to open his discussion with Kirsty with an attack on her approach, she would get defensive, and the argument would not be effective.

Lauren works at Bond Brothers, where she is a senior vice president. After her discussion with Jenny and Ray, she realizes that the approach to argument and challenge taken in her firm is really effective. But she feels that staff members at Bond Brothers are guilty of taking this approach for granted, and so she decides to give a presentation to remind everyone of how they should conduct healthy arguments.

See each extract from Lauren's presentation to review what she said.

Extract 1 - Rational

"Don't forget that arguments work best when people are rational. By that, I mean that you have to use facts, and if the other person is right, you have to accept it. It's OK to feel strongly, but don't hold on to an untenable position out of stubbornness."

Extract 2 - Personal

"Whatever you do, don't make arguments personal. Arguments should be about ideas, not the people who put them forward. Do not descend to saying negative things about co-workers when they're not around, personal abuse, stereotyping, and so on."

Extract 3 - Purposeful

"We argue for a purpose. That means that we don't argue just for the sake of arguing, or to score points. Our arguments must be productive. Remember that the goal of healthy argument is a solution that improves!"

Even after her presentation, Lauren is still worried that some of her managers don't seem to know how to encourage enough effective argument in their teams. So she sets up a master class for them, and calls in a manager who she knows has a positive approach to debate and discussion.

Lauren feels that hearing some real, live examples from within the company about people they know will show the managers how to encourage effective argument and challenge. Lauren asks Krista, the head of marketing, to describe how she makes debate work for Bond Brothers.

Krista: My story is about a debate that we had in my team about setting up a web site. You all know Eric, and how passionate he gets about Bond being better than other brokers. He felt that a web site was so predictable-- that we should show our difference and not use one.

Krista says in a friendly tone.

Lauren: So how did that work out in the team?

Lauren says, sounding interested.

Krista: You can imagine. Jess had created a sample site in her spare time, and researched rival sites. She looked like she was going to storm out when Eric started. But I just asked her about the numbers that show increased customer satisfaction from accessing products through a web site.

Krista says in a friendly tone.

Lauren: How did she react?

Lauren says, sounding interested.

Krista: She was brilliant. She gave Eric a lesson in the benefits of web site marketing. Everyone applauded, and he said that in that case, she was right to propose a web site. But then we started to talk about design. Jess showed her own example, and Eric said that he thought it was sloppy and amateurish.

Krista says in an explanatory tone.

Lauren: He's impossible!

Lauren says in an exasperated tone.

Krista: No, it was OK. I told him that he was being personal and offensive. He apologized to Jess, and then picked out what he liked about her sample site, and what he didn't. He showed her that the link to the tracker site was too complicated for customers to follow. He was right, and Jess altered it right there and then. It really improved the page.

Krista says in a reassuring tone.

Lauren: Good. Thanks for that, Krista. It's an inspiring tale about the way to manage arguments for the benefit of all.

Lauren says, sounding happy.

Lauren made a good choice in getting Krista to talk about her management of debate in her team. Krista made sure that the argument was rational by encouraging Jess to produce facts and figures to support her bid for a web site.

Krista even managed to keep Eric from personalizing the issue, and used his strengths to analyze the web site layout and suggest improvements. You can see that she really encouraged effective argument in her team.

If you follow Krista's example, then you'll also be able to encourage effective argument and challenge.

Promoting win-win solutions

When you think about conflict in the workplace, as in sport, the usual assumption is that if there is a winner, then there must also be a loser.

But you can reconfigure conflict situations in a way that makes everyone involved a winner.

Melvin is a waiter at Cootroute, a prestigious restaurant. Review his description of the way that conflict situations are handled in his organization.

A restaurant must seem to be a calm and organized place. But believe me, behind the scenes, it's very different. When you've got to get ninety meals out in the space of a few hours, tempers can fray.

But we worked out a long time ago that the way to operate is as a team.

That means that when we disagree with each other, we try to find a solution that works for both parties. Let me give you an example. Last week, we were three waiters down. That puts enormous pressure on everybody else. The chef was calling out orders, but there were not enough people to serve them.

In lots of kitchens, this would have caused a big shouting match. But when the kitchen staff saw the problem, they helped out by slowing down just enough for us to catch up. They didn't blame us, or try to make us look bad. They just helped.

In Melvin's restaurant, they are operating a win-win approach.

They succeed because they are:
- expressing a spirit of cooperation,
- exercising a high degree of trust between other parties,
- anticipating synergy--that the shared solution will be better than an individual win.

A win-win approach signals that the intention in the conflict is not to defeat the other side, but to collaborate to achieve a shared victory.

In Melvin's restaurant, they are operating a win-win approach.

Question

What three things do you need to do to promote win-win situations?

Options:
1. foster trust
2. defeat the other side
3. cooperate
4. aim for shared solutions

5. work alone
Answer:
Win-win solutions involve both parties trusting each other, being willing to cooperate, and working together towards shared solutions.

Option 1: This choice is correct. Building trust will promote a win-win situation. When both parties know they can rely on each other, they look for outcomes that benefit everyone involved.

Option 2: This option is incorrect. Defeating the other side is a win-lose situation in which one party wins and one party loses.

Option 3: This option is correct. Expressing a spirit of cooperation promotes a win-win situation because both parties work together to create an outcome that benefits everyone involved.

Option 4: This choice is correct. If both parties generate solutions that have mutually beneficial outcomes, they will promote a win-win situation.

Option 5: This option is incorrect. Working alone does not promote a win-win situation because there must be two parties involved to create a win-win situation.

Win-win solutions often occur because both parties realize that if they work together, they will gain. The parties also recognize that if they work against each other, often both sides lose.

Select each of the work issues for an example of how it is possible to create a cooperative and collaborative approach to conflict at work.

Pay rise
Rontech faced a claim from its workers for a substantial pay rise. The company felt that it would struggle to meet

these demands. The negotiated settlement was a pay rise, but it included provisos for extra productivity.

Locking up

Digicom had a conflict between two groups. When employees worked the weekend, security had to unlock and lock up after them. The solution: upon entry, staff members took keys from security and returned the keys upon exit.

Untidiness

Briony hated sharing an office with Vic. He was untidy, and always borrowed her stuff because he couldn't find his own. After an explosive argument, they agreed that Vic would purchase new equipment, but Briony would store it for him.

Outgoings

At Lena, the finance staff set a false claims deadline because they expected late claims. But employees ignored the false deadline, and expenses were always paid late. They all agreed to a real deadline, and people are now paid on time.

Win-win solutions cannot be imposed upon staff members. Both parties involved in any conflict must be willing to seek a mutually positive result.

If you want to promote win-win solutions to resolving conflict in the workplace, you need to apply three principles.

See each principle for a more detailed explanation of what it involves.

Avoid the zero-sum approach

The zero-sum approach is one in which the rewards of any negotiation are entirely given to one party. You must aim for a better allocation of rewards, so that all sides can gain from the solution. This may not result in actual equality, but it must be more equitable than the zero-sum idea.

Advocate flexible compromises

You need to be creative and flexible in identifying what you are trying to gain from the solution, and where you can compromise. A vital starting point is knowing what your bottom line is--the point below which you will not go.

Take a long-term perspective

One of the key principles of win-win approaches is that although in the short-term you might not achieve all that you wanted to, in the long-term you will gain more by being cooperative. You always gain something, whereas with an all-or-nothing approach you might get nothing.

Case Study: Question 1 of 1
Scenario

Julie works on the sixth floor. When she has visitors, the ground floor reception desk rings her to collect them. On days when she is hosting a meeting, it involves repeated journeys in the elevator.

Julie has asked that the receptionists just send people up, and she will meet them, but they refuse to do this on grounds of security. She calls the head of the reception services and comes to an agreement that she will notify reception of the participants of her meeting in advance, and they will hold them there until there is a sensible number to collect.

Answer the question about Julie's solution.

Question:

What rules of conduct to promote a win-win solution have Julie and her colleagues used?

Options:
1. They have avoided the zero-sum approach.
2. They have taken the long-term view.
3. They have achieved a flexible compromise.
4. Always negotiate with people at management level.

Answer:

Julie and her colleagues have achieved a win-win solution by applying the three core rules. They have avoided the zero-sum approach, they have been flexible, and been able to agree a compromise which is better for everyone in the long-term.

Option 1: This option is correct. Julie and her colleagues avoided the zero-sum approach by devising a solution in which both sides gained from the solution.

Option 2: This choice is correct. Julie didn't get exactly what she wanted, but she and her colleagues came up with a compromise in which they will gain more in the long-term by being cooperative.

Option 3: This is a correct choice. In creating their solution, Julie and her colleagues identified what each was trying to gain from the solution and struck a compromise with that in mind.

Option 4: Incorrect. Although Julie negotiated with the head of reception services, it is not always necessary to negotiate with people at a management level. Sometimes, a win-win solution can be best created by people at a lower level.

How can these principles be applied in the workplace? In the following example, you and Helen are representing your teams in talks over a merger. Both teams do the same work, but in different locations. Now they are to be merged into one team at head office.

Your job involves chasing the company's bad debtors for payment. The focus for the discussion is agreeing on the procedures that the new team will use. How can you best promote a win-win solution?

Case Study: Question 1 of 3
Scenario

For your convenience, the case study is repeated with each question.

You manage the drivers at Consento Trucking. The team is a real mix of people, and there are some long-standing personal antagonisms. This means that organizing shifts and work teams is very difficult. Consento has secured a new contract to organize the transport for a major pharmaceutical company.

You are going to use this opportunity to introduce a win-win approach to managing the team, and therefore reduce conflict.

Answer the questions, in order, to show how you will find win-win solutions.

Question:

Vitas is the charge hand on the small rigs, and Grant the charge hand on the large rigs. Some of the truckers are able to drive both types of rig. But Vitas in particular refuses to release any of his men to Grant. He organizes it so that they are always on a run if Grant wants them. You want these men available to Grant when they are needed. What should you do?

Options:

1. Take control of the allocation of runs.

2. Inform Vitas that Grant is now able to override his orders.

3. Order Vitas to release two drivers to Grant.

4. Instruct both Vitas and Grant that they must swap drivers when either needs to.

Answer:

You need to avoid a zero-sum solution of handing over complete control to Grant, or taking control yourself, and suggest something that allows both sides to gain or hold onto something.

Option 1: This choice is not correct because it requires that you to take control away from both Vitas and Grant. Both men lose if this solution is implemented.

Option 2: This is not correct because this approach is a zero-sum solution in which the rewards of the negotiation are entirely given to Grant. This is a win-lose solution that is likely to increase conflict between Vitas and Grant.

Option 3: This option is not correct because this is a zero-sum solution in which you take control and make a demand that benefits Grant but not Vitas. This strategy is likely to increase tension between Grant and Vitas.

Option 4: This is the best approach because it allows both Vitas and Grant to benefit from the solution. This is a much better approach than a zero-sum solution.

Case Study: Question 2 of 3

The budget is distributed between Grant and Vitas. Large trucks cost more, and so Vitas has always had the smaller share of budget. It is one of the major issues between him and Grant. How can you resolve this conflict over the budget to produce a win-win solution?

Options:

1. I can't. It may be hard on Vitas, but it is an economic fact of life.

2. I would split the budget directly down the middle, giving each half.

3. I would change the budget allocation to a monthly sum, so that the disparity between Vitas and Grant would appear to be less.

4. I would allocate a large part of the budget directly, but would reserve a portion so that both men could bid for extra sums for particular projects.

Answer:

You need to come up with a compromise which shows flexibility about identifying the gains from a different form of budget allocation. This supports a win-win solution.

Option 1: This option is incorrect because it is a rigid approach that does nothing to resolve the conflict between Grant and Vitas. This uncompromising position cannot produce a win-win solution.

Option 2: This option is incorrect because it produces a win-lose solution. It does not account for the greater expense of large trucks. This is a win for Vitas, but a loss for Grant.

Option 3: This choice is not correct because it does not address the problem to produce a win-win situation. A change in the allocation of the monies for the purpose of resolving the conflict is deceiving and may irritate Vitas even more.

Option 4: This choice is correct. This approach is a creative and flexible compromise that provides the opportunity for both men to benefit from this budget allocation. This facilitates a win-win solution.

Case Study: Question 3 of 3

Vitas feels disappointed by your approach. In his opinion, you are favoring Grant, and he feels that his position in the company is being undermined. What should you say to Vitas?

Options:

1. "I have to pick one side or the other, and Grant's area of work is the most valuable to the company."

2. "I will rotate your roles over the next few years to ensure that you reach the more important position."

3. "The large rig business is more lucrative right now. If you help Grant, the extra income from his section's growth will be spent on widening your distribution reach. You'll end up in a better position in the end."

4. "This is survival of the fittest. If you are not happy, fight back."

Answer:

To get Vitas' agreement, you need to point out how the win-win approach is a long-term strategy. The results that come from approaching conflict in this way even themselves out over time. This is better than keeping it as a competition.

Option 1: This option is incorrect because it supports the view that the only possible outcome is a win-lose solution. This comment will further alienate and anger Vitas, which may increase conflict on the team.

Option 2: This choice is incorrect. This comment promotes a win-lose solution in the long-term in which Vitas comes out ahead of Grant.

Option 3: Correct. To get Vitas's buy-in, you must convey that the win-win approach is a long-term strategy. You must acknowledge that although he may not achieve what he wanted in the short-term, in the long-term he will benefit more by being cooperative.

Option 4: This choice is not correct. This comment promotes conflict and supports a win-lose approach. The assumption here is that only the fittest wins.

Vitas and Grant can be managed in a way that fosters a win-win solution. The approach is to ensure that allocation of resources does not lead to a fixed and inequitable distribution.

By suggesting sensible compromises, both can find a measure of satisfaction. Both can come to see that, over time, they will benefit equally.

When you promote win-win solutions, you will find that people enjoy the benefits of this flexible and reasonable approach to conflict. After a while, everyone will recognize it as the most effective way to operate.

Recognizing Conflict

How much time is spent dealing with conflict in your workplace? Generally, you don't go to work to fight--you go to produce, and to earn. But some statistics suggest that people spend a lot of work time in conflict with each other.

In fact, some studies have suggested that between 30 percent and 40 percent of a manager's time is spent dealing with conflict. This amount of time away from productive work has serious cost implications.

Friction occurs when objects rub together, and results in a slowing down of their movement.

Friction in the workplace results from destructive conflict. It leads to the slowing down and seizing up of the interactions between people. It is therefore highlighted by some clear and recognizable signs.

One way to recognize destructive conflict in the workplace is to look at the extent of the rules and regulations that exist in an organization.

Rules and regulations are a necessary part of any organization, but in organizations which are suffering a lot of conflict, rules and regulations--open or hidden--will proliferate.

In many organizations, disputes between employees are managed easily, usually between the staff members themselves. But in organizations plagued by destructive conflict, this is not the case.

In these organizations, the resolution of differences is contentious, and seems to need the involvement of more and more people. This is described as escalating arbitration. So what does this mean? Think about it for a moment.

The signs of a destructive conflict

How much time is spent dealing with conflict in your workplace?

Generally, you don't go to work to fight--you go to produce, and to earn. But some statistics suggest that people spend a lot of work time in conflict with each other.

In fact, some studies have suggested that between 30 percent and 40 percent of a manager's time is spent dealing with conflict. This amount of time away from productive work has serious cost implications.

Question

Many people, and you may be one of them, view conflict in the workplace as an inevitable occurrence. They recognize that conflict has a cost in terms of time and distraction, but it is probably a price they would find hard to quantify.

What percentage of performance problems in the workplace do you think are caused by conflict?

Options:
1. 25%
2. 35%
3. 45%
4. 55%
5. 65%

Answer:

Option 1: You may be surprised to learn that according to Collaboration Works, an estimated 65 percent of performance problems are caused by conflict at work. Any reduction would therefore have a significant effect on workplace performance.

Option 2: You may be surprised to learn that according to Collaboration Works, an estimated 65 percent of performance problems are caused by conflict at work. Any reduction would therefore have a significant effect on workplace performance.

Option 3: You may be surprised to learn that according to Collaboration Works, an estimated 65 percent of performance problems are caused by conflict at work. Any reduction would therefore have a significant effect on workplace performance.

Option 4: You may be surprised to learn that according to Collaboration Works, an estimated 65 percent of performance problems are caused by conflict at work. Any reduction would therefore have a significant effect on workplace performance.

Option 5: You may be surprised to learn that according to Collaboration Works, an estimated 65 percent of performance problems are caused by conflict at work. Any reduction would therefore have a significant effect on workplace performance.

But not all conflict is detrimental, and most people agree that some conflict can have a positive and energizing effect on an organization. So the trick is to be able to recognize negative conflict. Then you can:

- distinguish between negative and positive conflict,
- be proactive in preventing negative conflict,
- deal with those aspects of conflict that are negative, and support the positive aspects.

Of course, the line between negative and positive conflict is a fine one, and may well be different in different situations. What might apply in one organization might not in another.

Question

Reuben and Sharon work in an organization characterized by conflict. Reuben says that it's the natural state of affairs. Sharon argues that something could be done if they could only identify the negative conflict. What benefits of this identification could she use to support her argument?

Options:

1. "We could then deal with the negative conflict, and support the positive."

2. "We can be proactive about preventing negative conflict."

3. "It will make the distinction between positive and negative conflict absolutely clear for all of our
   teams."

4. "We'll be able to distinguish between negative and positive conflict."

5. "We'll be able to get rid of conflict altogether."

Managing Workplace Conflicts

Answer:
By recognizing negative conflict, Sharon's organization will be able to deal with it, and proactively prevent it. Distinguishing between negative and positive conflict will help Sharon and her team to support the positive.

Option 1: This option is correct. Sharon should include this in her argument. If Sharon and her colleagues could identify the negative conflict, they could take steps to prevent it.

Option 2: This choice is correct. Sharon should use this point to support her argument. Being able to recognize negative conflict will help Sharon and her colleagues prevent it, which will create a healthier work environment.

Option 3: This is an incorrect choice. This is a point Sharon should omit from her argument. Although identifying negative conflict will make the distinction between positive and negative conflict clearer, it will never be totally clear for all teams.

Option 4: This is correct. This is a point that supports Sharon's position. Recognizing negative conflict will help Sharon and her colleagues make the distinction between positive and negative conflict, which will help prevent negative conflict.

Option 5: This option is incorrect. Sharon should not include this point in her argument because there is no way to eliminate conflict from organizations.

How you handle conflict is a contentious issue. Should you discourage conflict, or encourage it to energize your organization? Whatever you decide, one thing is certain--with the time that it consumes, conflict cannot be ignored.

Friction as a sign of conflict

Friction occurs when objects rub together, and results in a slowing down of their movement.

Friction in the workplace results from destructive conflict. It leads to the slowing down and seizing up of the interactions between people. It is therefore highlighted by some clear and recognizable signs. These are:
- ineffective communication,
- hostility between individuals,
- hostility between groups.

That is the situation at Sharon's place of work. Consider her description of the working conditions at Mirrorball Film Productions.

Sometimes I worry about going into work. If I'm on a project with Belle, it's fine, but if it's Clarice then I know it's going to be awful. We don't get along, and that's no good when we're the only two on the team. I've tried to make my peace with her, but she won't budge.

She got upset when I applied for acting senior auditor, and she didn't. She said that she wasn't informed that the position was vacant. I told her that if you waited around to be informed of everything, nothing would happen. You have to dig for information around here.

Anyway, I got the job, and for six months I was an auditor. Unfortunately, I had to check Clarice's accounts, and found a few discrepancies. Accountants don't like having their work checked by auditors at the best of times, but it has to be done. She's always gone out of her way to try to find fault with me as publicly as possible since then.

Sharon has described the signs of friction in the workplace. There is institutionalized conflict between groups in the organization--auditors and accountants--as well as personal antagonism between Sharon and Clarice.

Probably one of the causes of this is the poor communication system at Mirrorball. As Sharon says: "You have to dig for information around here."

But if you want to diagnose friction, you will need a more detailed breakdown of the symptoms associated with each sign.

See each sign of friction in the workplace to learn more about it.

Communication problems

Poor communication leads to poor coordination between parts of the workforce, and duplication of effort. Information may be held by one party and deliberately not given to others, or not sought, so that a lack of information can be used as an excuse for ignoring rules and regulations.

Group hostility

Groups may blame other groups, without justification, for their own problems. They may form temporary alliances to work against each other, or become so concerned with preserving their territories that they would rather fail than cooperate.

Personal hostility

Personal hostility makes all arguments personal, so that the focus is no longer on the real issues involved. Disagreements may escalate to include physical and verbal intimidation, often based on stereotyping and labeling.

See each symptom of friction for an example in the workplace.

Coordination

At a board meeting at Prestige Tooling, there was a major argument when the Vice President for Sites presented her plan for relocation of the Denver plant. The president had already commissioned external consultants to organize the move.

Information

Ron was more than satisfied when Corey made a fool of himself at the company sales rally. Ron hadn't told Corey about the new Anderson contract, so Corey didn't look too smart when he identified it as the next big target for his team.

Avoidance

Matt told his team that the new policy on energy efficiency meant carpooling whenever possible. Jade allowed her team to carry on using their own cars. No one told Jade that the policy meant carpooling, and she wasn't going to ask.

Blaming

When Ken's division was disciplined for overspending on new project planning software, he blamed the accountants for not allocating enough of a software budget. Ken approves all budget allocations.

Alliances

Security staff at CAT began randomly searching warehouse staff. Some were fired for stealing. Later, both groups resisted the introduction of surveillance cameras, which would mean less security personnel, but more security.

Stereotypes

The female staff at Exceed Engineering are a minority. They're used to being told that women don't make good engineers. But when Phil made a change to Sharon's design, everyone was shocked when she said he was "senile" for suggesting it.

Intimidation

Danny and Alan fought over their break times. Alan kept to time, but Danny took as long as he liked. Their arguments ended when Alan threw a notepad at Danny after one of his longest breaks, and they were moved to separate departments.

Question

Jefferson Bryant is a well-known real estate company. To its customers, it looks like a friendly and efficient organization. But behind the scenes, things are very different.

Match each symptom with a corresponding sign of friction.

Options:

A. Communication problems
B. Group hostility
C. Personal hostility

Targets:

1. Two staff members calling each other "cheats" over a sale that fails to go through. 2. The staff in accounts is not billing on time, as the salespeople don't update them. 3. A customer walking out as commercial and residential teams fight for the listing.

Answer:

Actually, the correct answers are indicated. Take another look at the "Symptoms of Friction" job aid by selecting the Job Aids button.

In this example, two staff members are exhibiting personal hostility. Their argument has become personal and is no longer focused on the real issues involved--a sale that fell through. The hostility has escalated to personal intimidation.

In this example, communication problems between departments are causing delayed billing. Salespeople are withholding information from the staff in accounts.

This is an example of group hostility. The teams were so busy preserving their territories that they lost a potential customer. They chose failure over cooperation.

Different organizations and teams deal with conflict in different ways.

See each team and consider what is happening in each. Try to diagnose the signs of friction.

Team A

Team A conducts telephone interviews for market research. The questionnaires are designed by another team. The two teams guard their responsibilities fiercely. Team A members have had to ask questions that they do not understand themselves.

Team B

Team B has just finished analyzing data from a survey of all sales teams. Team members had to chase the salespeople to get the data, so they were amazed when the Sales Director said that he produced a similar report six months ago.

Team C

Team C has a high turnover of staff. The team leader says that the problem lies in the sort of recruits that they have to accept. College graduates are too "soft and weak" to cope with the teasing that the older staff members employ.

Question

What is happening in each team? Match each sign of friction to the appropriate team.

Options:
A. Group hostility
B. Communication problems
C. Personal hostility

Answer:
In Team A there are territorial issues, whereas in Team B there is duplication of effort because of poor communication. In Team C the problem is that individuals are being stereotyped.

Team A is exhibiting signs of group hostility by guarding its territory to the detriment of the organization.

Team B is duplicating efforts because of communication problems between the team and the Sales Director. They failed to communicate about the sales report.

In Team C, there is personal hostility. The team leader is using verbal intimidation when stereotyping and labeling recruits as "soft and weak."

All of the teams described exhibit symptoms of friction. Team A is suffering from group hostility, failing to perform adequately because their question setters are being territorial. Team B has wasted time because the Sales Director actually had the vital information, but there was a breakdown in communication, and Team C doesn't even realize that people are being stereotyped offensively.

If productivity is suffering, look for the symptoms of communication issues, and group and personal hostility. They are the signs that you must watch for, because they signal conflict working destructively in your company.

Proliferating rules

One way to recognize destructive conflict in the workplace is to look at the extent of the rules and regulations that exist in an organization.

Rules and regulations are a necessary part of any organization, but in organizations which are suffering a lot of conflict, rules and regulations--open or hidden--will proliferate.

Control Systems is a typical organization with proliferating rules. Review how three employees describe what it is like to work there.

Annemarie: Sometimes it's difficult to understand what is acceptable here. Last week, a customer was pushing to know when he would get his order. And we're not supposed to tell customers that, just in case it's late. So I said that we couldn't guarantee a date, and he canceled.

Annemarie says in a defensive tone.

Bonnie: I know, it gets stupid sometimes. I was disciplined for wearing cropped pants. Apparently they are not trousers. Who says so? That's the first time that I've heard of it. I think that the managers just make the rules up as they go along.

Bonnie says in a defensive tone.

Dempsey: You know what I heard? We're going to be fined on the spot if they think that our desks are untidy. I don't think that's fair. There's a policy for everything here. Why can't they just trust us to do our jobs?

Dempsey says in a fed up tone.

Rules proliferate at Control Systems. They are constantly multiplying, and reproducing themselves in new forms.

The result is an organization clogged up with rules. The daily life of work becomes a process of weaving between rules and regulations that generally impede performance.

Employees get frustrated by the imposition of rules, and people who enforce the rules are challenged. Sometimes, rule enforcers insist on irrational adherence to rules, and people have to become rule breakers to get any work done.

Too many policies and regulations are a sign of a conflicted company. But there are also hidden rules and regulations. These are the norms, expectations, and even myths that exist in the workplace that control behavior.

See each type of rule to learn what characterizes each one.

Regulations

In conflict-laden organizations, there are often lots of little rules which concentrate on trivial matters, and impede performance.

Unofficial rules

Unofficial norms are not formally sanctioned, or often even known about by managers. They are intended to maintain the power of certain employees.

Three companies are given in which both official and unofficial rules have proliferated unnaturally. There are so many rules that all aspects of the working day are covered.

See each company to find out what employees have to say about the proliferating rules.

Stanton Steel

"Joe has run the tool room for twenty years. He insists that tools be returned each night, although they are booked out again by the same people the next morning. If you don't return them, then next time they are always unavailable."

St. Agnes Hospital

"We always get worried about doing rounds. Dressing professionally isn't a big deal, but it has gone too far now. After all, dress hardly affects our performances as doctors. One of my colleagues was even sent home because his tie wasn't knotted properly."

Maritime Insurance

"Nobody can remember why the policy exists, but we have to be in the office all day every Friday. But this only applies to the loss adjusters. Perhaps it used to be to catch up on paperwork, but it means that we have to pack all of our site visits into four days."

Question

Alison and Zak are discussing the proliferating rules in their organization. They've come up with a list of the rules that apply to them, and now they're trying to characterize them. Match each form of proliferating rules with one or more of its characteristics.

Options:

A. policies and regulations B. norms and myths
Targets:
1. intended to maintain individual employee power
2. not formally sanctioned
3. often concerned with trivial matters
4. too many can impede performance

Answer:

In conflict-laden organizations, policies and regulations tend to be concerned with trivial matters, impeding performance. Informal rules aren't formally sanctioned, and are intended to maintain individual power.

Norms and myths that exist in the workplace are intended to maintain the power base of certain individuals. This power often elevates the status of the person concerned.

Unofficial norms and myths are not formally sanctioned within an organization and may strongly influence staff behavior. Breaking these rules challenges the power of the group.

Some policies and regulations have little relevance or benefit to current organizational practices but are maintained out of a sense of caution, duty, or habit.

In conflict-ridden organizations, policies and regulations that focus on trivial matters rather than on meaningful ones can affect job performance and efficiency.

How will you recognize when rules are proliferating in an organization? See each type of organizational rule for more details about each one.

Performance

Some rules exist in a company due to habit. They have little or no relevance to current practices, but are maintained out of a misplaced sense of caution. With no logical foundation, they impede performance.

Unofficial

Unofficial rules may force the staff to behave in ways that they are unhappy about. Breaking these rules challenges the power of the group. Often they stem from patterns that some staff members liked, but that management has since discarded.

Trivia

Trivial rules are concerned with aspects of behavior that are irrelevant to performance. Peversely, ignoring these unimportant rules tends to result in major repercussions. They can be very annoying, and are easily used as weapons in workplace conflict.

Power

Many people use unofficial rules to develop a power base in organizations. Power raises the status of the person concerned, so these rules are often associated with long-serving lower status staff. Breaking these rules leads to further unofficial sanctions.

Is your organization suffering from proliferating rules, which are indicative of conflict?

Ask yourself the following questions to help you to identify the difference between necessary and proliferating rules. For example, are rules having an impact upon performance? Like Annemarie found at Control Systems, proliferating rules mean inefficient working practices. Do any of the following apply?

- Are there practices which have no official status, but, like being in the office on Fridays at Maritime Insurance, have become rules about the way you operate?
- Like the dress code at St. Agnes Hospital, do your rules focus on trivial matters, to the detriment of more significant concerns?
- Are there people like Joe at Stanton Steel in your organization? These people maintain their unsanctioned power through unofficial rules.

Managing Workplace Conflicts

The staff at the Miriam Plaza Hotel are about to walk out. When the owner Mary confronts them, they respond with a series of comments about the way that things are at the hotel. Four employees in particular have serious gripes about the behavior of the hotel manager, Mr. Allbright.

See each member of the staff for a comment.

Larry the bellboy
"Mr. Allbright says that I'm only allowed to carry one piece of luggage at a time. This means that I have to make at least two trips for each room, and the guests get really annoyed when their luggage takes so long to get to their rooms. He says it's hotel policy but I can't see why."

Zara from the kitchen
"How am I supposed to deal with room service requests when every sandwich has to be garnished differently from the last one? I don't think that guests compare sandwiches with each other. It's just stupid. I've had enough of it."

Jimmy the garage man
"I've told Allbright that I won't wear that stupid uniform. Garage staff are exempt from uniform regulations because none of the guests ever see them. I'm not letting him tell me what to wear."

Mrs. Kenton on reception
"That Allbright is a rogue. He knows that I decide on the uniform for the outdoor staff, not him. My husband used to be head porter, so I know what they should and shouldn't wear. I'll show Allbright he's not as important as he thinks he is."

Question
Which aspect of proliferating rules relates to which member of the staff from the hotel? Match each member of staff to the aspect of proliferating rules they relate to.

Options:
A. Zara from the kitchen
B. Mrs. Kenton on reception
C. Larry the bellboy
D. Jimmy the garage man

Targets:
1. rules which impede performance
2. unofficial rules
3. rules based on trivial concerns
4. rules intended to maintain unsanctioned power

Answer:

Zara is annoyed by a trivial rule, Larry's work is being impeded, Mrs. Kenton is focused on keeping her unofficial power, and Jimmy is annoyed about an unofficial rule that he does not feel that he must follow.

In the case of Larry the bellboy, the hotel's luggage policy impedes his performance and irritates customers. Without this policy, he could handle luggage more quickly and efficiently.

In the case of Jimmy, an unofficial rule that dictates what Jimmy wears has become law without being sanctioned. In fact, garage staff are exempt from uniform regulations. This unofficial rule is controlling staff behavior.

In Zara's case, she is burdened by a rule based on a trivial concern. There is no urgent customer need for every sandwich plate to be garnished differently, which makes the process much less efficient.

Mrs. Kenton is focused on keeping her unofficial power to decide on the uniforms for the outdoor staff. She is a lower-status person who is using a petty rule to make herself look more important.

Proliferating rules are a significant indicator of negative conflict. Now that you have identified the signs of them in the workplace, you will be able to eliminate them in your own organization.

Escalation of arbitration

In many organizations, disputes between employees are managed easily, usually between the staff members themselves. But in organizations plagued by destructive conflict, this is not the case.

In these organizations, the resolution of differences is contentious, and seems to need the involvement of more and more people. This is described as escalating arbitration. So what does this mean? Think about it for a moment.

See each situation for an explanation.

Arbitration

Arbitration is when individuals or groups at work seek out a third party to listen to their respective positions, and to make a decision on the situation.

Escalating arbitration

Escalation of arbitration is when conflict cannot be resolved, and must go to progressively higher and higher levels of authority for resolution.

After completing this topic, you should be able to

analyze a given situation to identify the reasons for the escalation of arbitration.

In many organizations, disputes between employees are managed easily, usually between the staff members themselves. But in organizations plagued by destructive conflict, this is not the case.

In these organizations, the resolution of differences is contentious, and seems to need the involvement of more and more people. This is described as escalating arbitration. So what does this mean? Think about it for a moment.

See each situation for an explanation.

Martin works in an organization in which there is escalating arbitration. He describes what happened to him.

It all started with Pattie's comment that I was too fat. I complained, and if she had just apologized then it would have ended there. But she wouldn't, and claimed that I'd called her a snob. My boss wanted me to say sorry, but

I really didn't see why she shouldn't apologize first. Then she threatened me with a lawsuit. My boss passed it over to the human resources director. She called us together to talk it through. I refused. Two women together--what chance did I stand?

Finally, the chief executive wrote to both of us, and said that as our relationship was so bad that we couldn't work together, he was relocating us to different offices. I'm not moving just because he can't solve a simple problem. I'm going to refuse. If he tries to make me, well, I've got lawyers, too.

As Martin's case shows, escalating arbitration occurs when two people cannot resolve their differences, and have to involve a third party--in this case, Martin's manager. But there were two further stages in this process for him.

See each stage to learn more about the process.

Stage 1

The decision went to a higher authority--the human resources director--but still a solution could not be devised.

Stage 2

Finally, the decision went to the chief executive. He tried to enforce a ruling, but Martin still resisted.

Even Martin can appreciate the stages of the failure to achieve a resolution of his differences with his co-worker.

I see now that if I'd been a bit more reasonable, and tried to make my peace with Pattie, then the situation wouldn't have escalated like it did. But neither of our bosses could get us to reach an agreement. Then it ended with the chief executive giving us an ultimatum.

Maybe I should have trusted the human resources director, but by then I wasn't thinking clearly. I'm looking to leave the company now, and so is Pattie. I think that we went too far.

In all companies, some disputes cannot be settled easily and amicably. Sometimes, people disagree and cannot reach a resolution. Sometimes, not even their immediate managers can resolve the situation. And so the arbitration escalates. But in organizations characterized by destructive conflict, the attitudes of people disagreeing with each other is different from that in organizations where conflict is a healthy force.

Question
What is the definition of escalation of arbitration?

Options:
1. when conflict can be resolved, but goes higher up the organization for ratification
2. when conflict cannot be resolved, and goes higher and higher up the organization for resolution
3. when conflict cannot be managed, and the decision goes outside of the organization

Answer:

Escalation of arbitration is when conflict cannot be resolved, and goes higher and higher up the organization for some sort of resolution.

Option 1: This is not the correct definition of escalation of arbitration. This definition describes an approval process, not a conflict-resolution process.

Option 2: This choice is correct. When you can't resolve your conflict, you may have to take it to someone higher in the organization. This is known as escalation of arbitration.

Option 3: This is not the definition of escalation of arbitration because this process involves going outside an organization. Escalation of arbitration is a conflict-resolution process that occurs within an organization.

In organizations in which there is destructive conflict, escalating arbitration is characterized by the following:
- protagonists ignoring the greater good,
- game playing on the part of both parties,
- assumptions that everyone is operating out of self-interest.

Martin's boss, Lee, doesn't see Martin and Pattie's behavior as indicating a positive attitude towards conflict.

Both of them were unreasonable. I asked Pattie to apologize, and I think that she might have. But Martin just refused. He wanted to make as much of it as he could, and I think that Pattie just joined in to make more mischief.

Nothing I said seemed to have any effect. They were really suspicious of my motives. I suppose that they thought I was secretly favoring one of them. It caused so much trouble. Everybody's work suffered, but they didn't seem to care.

As Lee discovered, the attitudes of both Martin and Pattie did not allow the dispute to be resolved easily.

Neither of them were troubled that their game playing was having an adverse effect on the rest of the staff.

Lee's attempts at resolving the conflict also failed, because their attitude toward him was based on the assumption that his motives were as suspect as their own.

In most organizations where arbitration escalates, it is because the protagonists genuinely value their own points of view. In organizations where this signals negative conflict, the attitudes of protagonists toward the disputes are more destructive and devious.

See each characteristic of escalating arbitration for more information.

The greater good

The protagonists are unwilling to change for the greater good. They are self-centered, and will not be flexible for the good of the work community. They want the results to be entirely in their favor, and they have complete disregard for the impact that the situation has on everyone else.

Game playing

Disagreements provide opportunities for game playing. The games played are things like arguing just for the sake of it, seeking unreasonable compromises from others, and willful contradictions made to annoy others. Arguments become opportunities to make mischief.

Self-interest

Arbitration escalates when no one believes anyone else. All parties are assumed to be operating out of pure self-interest, and anything that arbitrators suggest is seen as being for their own benefit. Arbitrators are often disparaged, and their recommendations ignored.

Case Study: Question 1 of 1

Scenario

Julie liked working in the back office as it was relaxed, and she could listen to music on her headphones. Bill, at the next desk, complained that it was disturbing his work. Bill asked Terri, the supervisor, to intervene, but when she told him not to make trouble, he assumed it was gender bias.

The office split down age lines--older people supporting Bill--and cooperation declined. Nobody could get anyone to compromise--and Julie even turned the music up. Then John, from the head office, came to see why output had fallen, and banned all music.

Answer the question that follows.

Question

Which options identify the attitudes of the people involved?

Options:

1. Julie was not concerned about the greater good.
2. Both parties were trying to achieve an amicable solution.
3. Once the dispute started, game playing began.
4. Bill assumed that Terri was acting out of self-interest.

Answer:

Julie was unwilling to accept the impact of her music and the argument on productivity. Once it began, the whole office got in on the disagreement. Terri was hurt by the assumption that even arbiters have dubious motives. No one wanted an amicable solution!

Option 1: This option is correct. After Bill told Julie that her music was affecting his productivity, Julie was unwilling to change her behavior. She displayed self-centered behavior and would not be flexible for the good of the work community.

Option 2: This is not a correct choice. No one wanted to compromise to achieve a workable solution for the office. In the end, everyone suffered.

Option 3: This option is correct. The office dispute spawned game playing. An age-based rift emerged, and no one was willing to compromise. It seemed as if people were joining in on the conflict just for the sake of it.

Option 4: This option is correct. Bill made an assumption that Terri was motivated purely by self-interest, so he wouldn't accept her arbitration. He assumed that she was aligning with Julie because of a gender bias.

Now consider the situation at Evernice Biscuits, and analyze the problems there as you did with your interviews with Martin and Pattie.

Case Study: Question 1 of 3

Scenario

For your convenience, the case study is repeated with each question.

You have been called in as a consultant to Evernice Biscuits, a large producer of quality confectionery. The director of human resources has become particularly concerned about the design and packaging

department.

She describes the atmosphere as poisonous. There are a lot of complaints lodged by the staff against colleagues and management that never seem to be resolved easily.

Your task is to investigate the situation, and to identify what the problem is. Do this by answering the following questions in order.

Question

June has recently changed offices, and is in a dispute with her co-workers about the office layout. She insists on being nearest the window, so that she can "see nature" for inspiration.

The others are challenging this. They say they want to sit together because it is better feng shui. June offers to bend down when they want to talk, so she won't obstruct their view of one another.

How would you characterize this behavior?

Options:

1. This is game playing. June's compromise is frivolous.
2. June is offering a reasonable compromise.
3. June is being difficult. Her co-workers are being reasonable.
4. June's co-workers are provoking her into continuing the argument by being difficult.

Answer:

This is indeed game playing. June's compromise was designed to be rejected in order to continue the dispute, and using feng shui to provoke the argument is playing games, too.

Option 1: This option is correct because June's compromise was unreasonable and made to annoy her co-workers.

Option 2: This option is not correct because June's compromise is unreasonable. To offer to bend down every time her co-workers want to talk is simply goading them to continue the dispute.

Option 3: This choice is incorrect because both parties are being unreasonable and playing games. Neither June nor her co-workers offer an acceptable compromise. Each side seems to want to incite the other.

Option 4: This choice is correct. June's co-workers are playing games by using a frivolous argument about feng shui made to annoy her.

Case Study: Question 2 of 3

The packaging department has an ongoing dispute with marketing. Rick, the chief designer, has told his staff to refuse to discuss the packaging with their colleagues in marketing. The marketing people have a design that they know Rick would like, but refuse to show it to him because he has upset them so many times in the past. The product launch date aimed for the Frankfurt Food Fair has been missed.

What sort of behavior is recognizable in this situation?

Options:

1. Rick's high standards are preventing him from compromising.

2. No one is acting for the greater good of the company.

3. Rick's behavior stems from the fact that product packaging should be controlled by marketing.

4. The marketing people are being difficult for the sake of it.

Answer:

This is a clear example of lack of concern for the greater good. The dispute is more important than meeting the deadline, and the marketing people are just enjoying the argument.

Option 1: This option is incorrect. Rick's high standards aren't preventing him from compromising; his department's dispute with the marketing department is.

Option 2: Correct. Neither the packaging department nor the marketing department is concerned with the greater good of the company. Neither is willing to be flexible for the good of the work community. As a result, the product launch date was missed.

Option 3: This choice is not correct. As the chief designer in the packaging department, Rick would not want product packaging to be controlled by marketing. His behavior stems from a ongoing dispute with marketing.

Option 4: This is correct. Because of the rift between the two departments and historical problems with Rick, the marketing department is withholding a design from him. The marketing department is arguing for the sake of it.

Case Study: Question 3 of 3

Alvin from sales tried to intervene to meet the deadline, with a suggested interim package style that he designed. Alvin had previously proposed a company restructure in which design and marketing would be subsumed by sales. When he submitted his interim package style, both the marketing and design people said it was unworkable, without looking at it properly.

What is the most likely explanation for what is going on here, based on what you know?

Options:

1. Alvin did not have the expertise to offer a sensible suggestion.

2. Alvin was game playing, just to make things worse.

3. Alvin was rejected because neither side could trust him. They assumed that he was only acting out of self-interest.

4. The marketing people were jealous, and wanted recognition.
Answer:
Since he had suggested the takeover of both departments, both sides assumed that Alvin was acting out of self-interest.

Option 1: This option is incorrect. There is not enough information to make this assessment. It is possible that Alvin did have the background to put forth a reasonable solution.

Option 2: This option is not correct. Alvin was not playing games. He intervened when the packaging and marketing departments were at a standstill. He proposed a package solution that would help the company meet the deadline.

Option 3: This choice is correct. Both departments were suspicious of Alvin's motives. They assumed he was acting out of self-interest because of the restructuring he had proposed in the past. Therefore, they rejected his recommendation.

Option 4: Jealousy is not the likely explanation for the marketing department's behavior. If recognition was what they wanted, they would have shown their package design. Instead, they withheld their design.

Evernice shows some clear signs of escalating arbitration. June plays games, and her colleagues join in, so that their argument is bound to continue. Both Rick and the marketing department argue for the sake of it, and put self-interest first.

Alvin's attempts to help are doomed by the belief that his motives are related to office politics.

Sorin Dumitrascu

No organization is free of disputes which need resolving. But the escalating arbitration that occurs in organizations suffering from destructive conflict involves certain warning signs--and now you can recognize them.

CHAPTER TWO
Handling Conflict

Your Attitude Towards Conflict

Trying to deal with conflict without being aware of your instinctive responses is like shooting an arrow with your eyes closed . You'll probably hit something, but will it be your intended target?

Everyone has a slightly different view on conflict. Consider Inez and Stan for example; they have widely differing views about conflict.

It's a basic rule of psychology that if you want to change your behavior, you have to understand what you're doing now. Your current behavior likely falls into one of five instinctive approaches to conflict, which are: fearful, problem solving, compromising, withdrawing, and overpowering. Understanding your current behavior applies in many situations, but never more so than when dealing with conflict.

Conflicts evoke instinctive responses. But once people move beyond instinct, they can choose which approach to take when disputes arise.

One way to consider this is to think about the desire to be cooperative compared to the desire to be assertive. Tom and Kelsey are both managers, and they're in the middle of an acrimonious discussion about how to stop people from arriving late for work.

Personal attitudes

Trying to deal with conflict without being aware of your instinctive responses is like shooting an arrow with your eyes closed .

You'll probably hit something, but will it be your intended target?

Conflicts are times of emotion and stress. Gina is thinking about how a recent encounter with a colleague made her feel.

Gina: I feel so angry with myself. When she attacked me verbally, I just lost it. I couldn't speak properly--I was blushing and stammering, and I forgot everything that I'd planned to say. It was awful.

Gina was surprised by the depth and power of her emotions in the face of conflict. If she'd been more self-aware, and taken the time to reflect on her instinctive approaches to conflict, she could have:

- prepared herself for her emotional reaction,
- mastered her emotions,
- devised an alternative, more effective approach.

A conflict involves two people, so how the other person behaves affects your emotions. Gina felt attacked, which made her then feel insecure.

In such cases, it is hard to anticipate and master your instinctive feelings. But if you can, you will probably deal with the situation more effectively.

Harry has the opposite problem to Gina. He isn't frightened by conflict, but he still avoids it. He had a bad experience during an argument in his last workplace, and now people think that he's weak because he avoids getting involved.

Question

Harry has missed out on a promotion because he isn't assertive enough. To help Harry to get a promotion in the future, his supervisor advises him to become aware of his attitudes about conflict. How could Harry benefit from doing this?

Options:

1. Harry could apply a more effective approach to conflict.

2. Harry could control the behavior of the other person involved in the conflict.

3. Harry would be prepared for his overreaction to conflict.

4. Harry would be able to master his emotions.

5. Harry would be able to ensure that he didn't get involved in any conflict.

Answer:

Moving beyond an instinctive approach to conflict is only possible with self-awareness. If Harry can do this, he'll be able to be prepared for his reactions, master his emotions, and apply different approaches to conflict.

Option 1: This choice is correct. If Harry were to reflect on his instinctive approaches to conflict, he could approach conflict in a more effective way and, as a result, have more success at work.

Option 2: This option is not correct because it is very difficult to control others' behavior, whether you're in a conflict or not. Harry only has control over his own behavior.

Option 3: This choice is correct. Harry, like many people, has a strong reaction to conflict. If he were to learn about his attitudes to conflict, he could be ready for his strong reaction and take control of his approach to conflict.

Option 4: This is correct. If Harry learned about his attitudes to conflict, he could gain mastery over his emotional reaction. That way, when conflict arose, his emotions wouldn't control him.

Option 5: This choice is incorrect. There is no way for Harry to completely eliminate conflict from his life. He can learn to manage it when it arises, but he can't control whether it occurs.

Conflict often arouses an instinctive, rather than intellectual, response. Identify these instincts, and your intelligence can begin to take control of your approach to conflict.

Learning about conflict

Everyone has a slightly different view on conflict. Consider Inez and Stan for example; they have widely differing views about conflict.

- "I definitely agree with my grandmother on this. She used to say that it is easier to refrain from than retreat from an argument."
- "There are two kinds of people in the world--the winners and the losers. If I get into an argument, I aim to win!"

Inez and Stan have polarized views about conflict. Whenever you compete with or disagree with people, your behavior will probably fall somewhere on a continuum between these extremes.

So, do you back off from an argument easily, or do you have to win at all costs? Jim and Harriet have different attitudes about their disagreements with each other.

Jim: I hate it when we fight. Why are you always arguing? It doesn't get us anywhere, and you always have to win. One day, we'll fight so much that we won't be able to make up.

Harriet: You need to learn to stand up for yourself. You always give in too quickly, when I know that you don't agree with me. I believe in what I say, and I'm willing to fight for it. I think on my feet. When someone disagrees with me, then I get really involved.

The contrast here is between Jim, who fears the effects of conflict, and Harriet, who relishes a good argument. But how do such attitudes about conflict develop? There are two forces at work:

- family upbringing
- national culture

As you experience conflict throughout your life, you may moderate and perhaps control your instinctive childhood responses.

But the power of instinct should not be underestimated. At times of stress, most people will still react without thinking. This is when your ingrained responses will emerge most powerfully.

Experiences before the age of seven are particularly influential on attitudes later in life. People experience a huge range of conflict in childhood, from disagreements about television to acrimonious divorce. Young children soak all this up, and this may have profound impacts on how they deal with conflict as adults.

See each person to reveal their stories about conflict.

Marie

"I used to hear my mom and dad arguing all the time. When they broke up, they argued about who I was going to live with. I hated it. I didn't want to be the cause of more fights, so now I just avoid all conflict."

Ian

"In our house, my parents argued a lot. It sounded awful, but then they made up. They always ended up being happy with each other, so conflict doesn't really scare me now."

Poppy

"I grew up with three brothers, so I had to stand up for myself. Nobody gave in to me. My mom used to call me 'the baby,' but my brothers didn't see it that way. I still think that I need to fight to get what I want, even now."

Celine

"When I was little, I used to have temper tantrums. If I yelled long enough and loud enough, my parents always gave in. It still works with people now!"

Marie's experiences told her that conflict only ever leads to unhappiness. Now she avoids it, even though this causes her problems. Poppy has carried the competitiveness of her childhood right through her life. She is a successful lawyer with a reputation for trouble-shooting. Celine's colleagues see her as a spoiled brat-- she's not very popular. But Ian has learned that you can have a good argument and still get along well with people.

Geert Hofstede investigated the way that national culture influences behavior. One aspect of his analysis, which is relevant to conflict in the workplace, is the extent to which cultures are collectivist or individualistic. Collectivist cultures are ones in which the interests of the group prevail over the interests of the individual. Individualist cultures have the opposite view.

See each kind of culture to learn how it affects attitudes towards conflict.

Collectivist

These cultures believe that harmony should always be maintained, and direct confrontations avoided. The word "no" is seldom used, because it is confrontational. Instead, they say: "You may be right."

Individualistic

In these cultures, speaking your mind is a virtue. People believe that a clash of opinions leads to a higher truth. Telling the truth, even if it hurts other people, is considered to be the right thing to do.

According to Hofstede, the US epitomizes the individualistic type of culture, and Far East countries are examples of collectivist cultures.

Question

Fujio, Sybil, Ellen, and Mark are discussing how their different attitudes towards conflict have developed. Who is correctly identifying the factors that determine attitudes towards conflict?

Options:

1. Fujio believes that attitudes in society have a lot of influence over attitudes about conflict.

2. Sybil argues that attitudes about conflict are dictated by genes.

3. Ellen thinks that attitudes about conflict come from family upbringing.

4. Mark believes that attitudes to conflict are based upon primitive instincts.

Answer:

The most powerful factors determining attitudes to conflict are family upbringing and national culture. Although some people argue that genes play a role, this view is not widely accepted.

Option 1: This is correct. Fujio's view is widely supported. Attitudes are learned behaviors and are influenced by culture and society. The same is true about attitudes towards conflict. National culture shapes the way people think about conflict.

Option 2: This is not a correct choice. Sybil's view is not supported by research. There is not much evidence to support the position that genetic makeup determines attitudes towards conflict.

Option 3: This choice is correct. Ellen's view that family upbringing determines attitudes towards conflict is widely supported. The way in which conflict is viewed and approached in families influences attitudes later in life.

Option 4: Mark's belief is not correct. Although reactions to conflict may be based on primitive instincts, attitudes towards conflict are not. Attitudes are learned responses.

If you want to be effective in handling conflict, then you have to be able to move beyond your instinctive responses. That means you need to pinpoint where they come from, and establish how powerful a factor they are.

How do you handle conflict?

It's a basic rule of psychology that if you want to change your behavior, you have to understand what you're doing now. Your current behavior likely falls into one of five instinctive approaches to conflict, which are: fearful, problem solving, compromising, withdrawing, and overpowering. Understanding your current behavior applies in many situations, but never more so than when dealing with conflict.

People handle conflict instinctively. In other words, they act without thinking. So to change that behavior, they must think carefully, openly, and honestly about their responses.

When two people are in a dispute, how they react depends upon their attitudes to two main elements: goals and relationships.

See each element to discover more about how it relates to conflict.

Goals

Your goals are the results that you want from the dispute. How important are these goals? Will you do whatever it takes to achieve them?

Relationships

How important is your relationship with the other person in the dispute? Do you both need to remain on good terms?

The goal and relationship elements are in a constant state of tension during conflicts. How you manage one will affect the other. But they can both be managed successfully.

Yesterday, Juan and Kate argued about when to take their vacations. Today, after they've cooled down, they are talking about what happened.

Kate: I hated how you had to get your own way. I thought that we were friends. You could have thought more about my needs.

Juan: I'm sorry, but that holiday is important to me. I want to go to my sister's wedding, and I need that time off. So friendship is less important than family this time.

Question

In their conversation, Juan and Kate displayed the main concerns that people have when in a conflict situation. What are these concerns?

Options:

1. relationships
2. looks
3. reputations
4. goals

Answer:

In fact, the main two concerns are about getting the best result, and maintaining a good relationship with the other person.

Option 1: Correct. Relationships are of primary concern during a dispute. Relationships are in a constant state of tension during a conflict. The importance of the relationship will influence the behavior of the people involved in a conflict.

Option 2: This choice is not correct. Although looks may be a concern for some people, they are not the main concern in a conflict situation. In a conflict situation, other factors take precedence.

Option 3: This option is incorrect. Concern over reputation may factor into a conflict situation, but is not one of the main concerns. Reputation is not necessarily at stake during a conflict.

Option 4: This choice is correct. One of the primary concerns during a conflict are the goals or outcomes one seeks to achieve. The importance of the outcome will influence one's behavior during the dispute.

So how do you balance your concern about achieving your goal with your concern about the relationship? See each approach to conflict for a description. Can you recognize how a category applies to you?

Fearful

You don't like conflict because it means that people won't like you, and you want to be liked. So when you are in a conflict situation, the other person's view of you is more important than winning the argument.

Problem solving

You see conflict as a problem to be solved, with both sides equally involved. You will not be satisfied with a half-hearted solution, but will push for a decision that is synergistic. You see conflicts as opportunities.

Compromising

You believe in a shared approach to conflict--that if both sides give and take, then everybody will be happy.

Withdrawing

You withdraw from conflict situations, and will give in rather than argue. During conflicts, you feel anxious and unhappy, because you feel that the outcome is always bad for you.

Overpowering

You have to have your way. If this means damaging the relationship with the other person, then so be it. Your tactics involve overpowering the opposition, and sometimes even using intimidation.

Question

Arthur is having problems with his team members. They all seem to handle conflict in very different ways, and so there is a lot of tension within the team. Help Arthur to understand what is happening by matching each approach to conflict with the statement that best summarizes it .

Options:
A. fearful
B. problem solving
C. compromising
D. overpowering
E. withdrawing

Targets:
1. You like a shared approach to conflict.
2. You overwhelm the opposition.
3. You care about someone's opinion more than winning.
4. You give in to people and avoid conflict.
5. You see conflicts as opportunities.

Answer:

By understanding that there are five distinct ways to deal with conflict, Arthur should be able to relieve the tension in his team.

This is the compromising approach to conflict. You believe in a collaborative approach, that if both sides give and receive, then everybody will be pleased with the results.

This is the overpowering approach to conflict. You must have your way at all costs. Your tactics involve overpowering the opposition and sometimes even using intimidation. Winning is more important than preserving relationships.

This is the fearful approach to conflict. You dislike conflict because it means that people may not like you. Being liked is more important than winning an argument.

This is the withdrawing approach to conflict. You are averse to conflict and will withdraw from conflict situations. Conflicts make you feel anxious because you feel that the outcome is always bad for you.

This is the problem-solving approach to conflict. You see conflict as an opportunity and a problem to be solved, with both sides equally involved. You push for a decision that is synergistic.

Now that you know more about your instinctive approach to conflict, you can begin to develop better ways of handling it when it occurs.

Approaches to conflict

Conflicts evoke instinctive responses. But once people move beyond instinct, they can choose which approach to take when disputes arise.

One way to consider this is to think about the desire to be cooperative compared to the desire to be assertive. Tom and Kelsey are both managers, and they're in the middle of an acrimonious discussion about how to stop people from arriving late for work.

Kelsey: We have to be sensitive about this. Only a few people have a problem. We shouldn't treat everyone as though we don't trust them to arrive on time.

Tom: I don't agree. I know these people, and nothing will change unless we install a time clock, and make them use it.

Kelsey: A time clock might be a good idea, but what about starting with everybody just signing in? That would make them think about the time that they arrive. It's also less draconian than a time clock.

Tom: No way. We must have a time clock.

Kelsey: Listen, I agree with you that there is a problem, but only with a few people. Why don't I speak to them first, and see what effect that has?

Tom is being competitive, whereas Kelsey is being collaborative by accepting Tom's idea, but modifying it. These positions are two of the five possible ways to approach conflict. The five approaches differ according to how much assertiveness and how much cooperation is shown.

See each approach to a conflict for a description.

avoidance

This is unassertive and uncooperative behavior. It involves abdicating any responsibility for the outcome of the conflict, and ignoring your own interests and the interests of the other party, leaving it to "fate."

accommodation

This is behavior that is cooperative but unassertive. If you follow this path, you will ignore your own interests in favor of the other person's interests. But then you are surrendering, which can be frustrating in the long term.

acceptance

This approach involves nearly equal parts of assertiveness and cooperation, but cooperation is slightly higher. You sacrifice some of your own aims to reach an outcome that is minimally acceptable to you both. You lose more than you gain, but you do gain.

collaboration

This approach is equal in terms of cooperation and assertiveness, and you attempt to maximize the gains of both parties. It is different from acceptance, which involves a minimal solution. Using the collaboration approach, you try to find the best result for all.

competition

This approach is the triumph of assertiveness over cooperation. At the extreme end of this spectrum, the desire to achieve your goal can make you ruthless and inconsiderate. There is no attempt to find any form of joint solution.

Briony and Denzel now join Tom and Kelsey in the argument about the late arrival of employees.

Briony: Why don't you guys calm down! I agree with Tom--we definitely need a time clock. But how about trying signing in for a while, and then, if that doesn't work, resorting to the time clock idea?

Denzel: I was going to suggest that we send a memo around to everyone, but Briony's idea is fine.

In the meantime, Sam has approached the group.

Denzel: What do you think, Sam?

Sam: Don't ask me, I don't want to get involved.

Tom: OK. So, we all agree to the time clock idea, huh?

Kelsey: No, Tom, we don't all agree to that. The best temporary solution is to get them to sign in, and to speak to the main culprits. If that doesn't work, we'll get a time clock.

Through her collaborative approach, Kelsey has suggested a good solution to the problem that seeks to satisfy everyone. Tom, however, is maintaining his competitive stance. Briony is taking the acceptance route, as she actually agrees with Tom, and so will be losing more than she gains by agreeing with Kelsey. Denzel seems happiest to sacrifice his own ideas, so he is taking an accommodation stance. Sam is avoiding the whole discussion--he obviously feels uncomfortable with any form of conflict.

Question

How do the five approaches relate to assertiveness and cooperation? Match each approach with its correct description.

Options:

A. accommodation
B. acceptance
C. avoidance
D. collaboration
E. competition

Targets:

1. unassertive and uncooperative
2. cooperative but unassertive
3. equal amounts of cooperation and assertiveness
4. a triumph of assertiveness over cooperation
5. nearly equal, but slightly more cooperation

Answer:

Competition is assertive and uncooperative, avoidance is neither assertive nor cooperative, acceptance is nearly equal but slightly more cooperative, accommodation is unassertive but cooperative, and collaboration involves both equally.

Unassertive and uncooperative behavior characterizes the avoidance approach. It involves relinquishing responsibility for the outcome of the conflict and ignoring one's own interests and the interests of the other party.

When someone is cooperative but unassertive, she is exhibiting the accommodation approach. A person who takes this approach ignores her own interests in favor of the other person's interests.

The collaboration approach is equal in terms of cooperation and assertiveness, and an attempt is made to maximize the gains of both parties. The person using the collaboration approach tries to find the best result for all.

The competitive approach is the triumph of assertiveness over cooperation. The desire to achieve one's own goal can make a person ruthless, inflexible, and inconsiderate. There is no attempt to reach a collaborative solution.

The acceptance approach involves nearly equal parts of assertiveness and cooperation, but cooperation may be slightly higher. You sacrifice some of your goals to achieve an outcome that is minimally acceptable to both sides.

So you now have a considerable repertoire of ways to approach conflict. But when should you use these different approaches?

See each approach again to see the different circumstances that will help you to decide which approach to use.

Competition

Use competition when speed is crucial, or when the other party would take advantage of the situation if you didn't compete. Competition is the best approach when the decision is vital to your survival.

Collaboration

Use a collaborative approach when you need to gain the commitment of the other party. Collaboration works well when the feelings and emotions of all parties need to be explored, and you have plenty of time.

Acceptance

Use an acceptance approach when the parties involved are equal, and a stalemate is likely. This approach works well when a temporary settlement is needed, and collaboration and competition would not work.

Avoidance

Use an avoidance approach when there is no need for an immediate decision, and more information is required to make the decision. Avoidance is useful when emotions are running too high and a more competitive approach would result in loss for all.

Accommodation

Accommodation is a suitable approach when you are in the wrong, and when the impact upon the other party is more important than the impact upon you.

Now you can explore some examples of these approaches to conflict. See each company to learn how each one has applied a different approach to conflict in the workplace.

Premier Software

The employees developing new software for an accounting contract couldn't agree on the design. Tempers flared, and until the client clarified his requirements, the manager decided to avoid further conflict until people cooled down.

James Noon and Sons

Jimmy Noon wasn't known for being decisive, but when a takeover of his company loomed, he rushed to buy back a majority share, ignoring the other options that his son suggested. There was no way that he was giving up his company without a fight.

The Rodhopper Press

Employees were prewarned about the new working conditions, so that they had time to discuss them with their managers. To get their collaboration, the managers were happy to take the time to find a mutual solution to the loss of traditional printing jobs.

GBC Inc.

In deciding whether to promote either Alex or Ryan, the chief executive took an acceptance route, by suggesting a job share arrangement. They were equal, and a stalemate was likely. A temporary solution would give him time to see which one emerged as the better permanent candidate.

Prentice and McCabe

Mary Prentice realized that she had misjudged how important the decision to get a new business partner was to her partner, Tom McCabe. So she backed down to accommodate his needs. After all, he had the biggest workload, and needed the extra person more than she did.

Conflict Handling Techniques

There's no doubt that when conflict isn't managed correctly, it can be a very destructive force. Destructive conflict is seen as the norm in some workplaces, and no one even tries to manage it. In these cases, it's hard for employees to imagine life without conflict.

Have you ever avoided conflict, or overreacted in a conflict situation? Although avoiding conflict or being competitive seem like sensible options, they are both problematic responses.

If you avoid conflict, you're only stockpiling trouble. Losing your temper is easy, and sometimes instinctive, but although you might initially overwhelm your colleagues, in the end they will look for revenge.

When groups or individuals fail to communicate, they often find themselves in conflict. And when they are in conflict, they often fail to communicate. So communication problems are both the cause and the result of conflict in the workplace.

Therefore, communication skills are a vital element of your conflict handling repertoire. Communication is concerned with understanding other points of view. If you can't see things from someone else's viewpoint, then your positions become more and more polarized.

Imagine that you're racing for the only available parking space when somebody cuts in front of you and parks. You have an argument about it, neither person listening to or caring about the other's feelings. So what's the difference between this scenario and conflict at work?

The difference is that you'll probably never see that stranger again, but you have to continue working with your colleagues. Ongoing relationships affect the outcome of arguments.

Applying techniques to handle conflicts

There's no doubt that when conflict isn't managed correctly, it can be a very destructive force.

Destructive conflict is seen as the norm in some workplaces, and no one even tries to manage it. In these cases, it's hard for employees to imagine life without conflict.

But destructive conflict can be managed. Cassie shows how this happened in her office.

Managing Workplace Conflicts

Cassie: We hated the auditors, and everybody spent their time fighting each other over the dumbest things. But that was how it always was. At the end of quarter, the tension was awful. But now the area director has helped us to confront and resolve our differences. I've realized that the auditors are really nice people!

Cassie's experience shows how much better life at work can be without constant destructive conflict.

But to manage it well, you need to: • confront the conflict

• communicate with the other party • agree to a solution.

Conflict involves strong emotions. People often lose their tempers when trying to deal with each other. Though emotions rarely resolve conflicts, calm minds can.

If conflict results in one side gaining at the expense of the other, the resolution is usually temporary. The loser will try to fight again. But if conflict is resolved to the satisfaction of both sides, then that conflict is over.

The techniques taught in this lesson are simple, but they can have magical results. If conflict in your workplace has been ignored or dealt with badly, you can apply these techniques, and benefit in several ways:

- Conflict will be turned from a destructive force into a constructive force.
- You can manage conflict rationally, not emotionally.
- All parties in the conflict can be winners.

These techniques won't always make you popular. When conflict is seen as normal, you may upset both the "avoiders" of conflict and the "shouters" at first. But the situation will get better.

Question

Cassie now knows that, handled properly, conflict can change the atmosphere in a workplace. How can she benefit from applying techniques to handle destructive conflict better?

Options:

1. All of the parties in the various conflicts can be winners.
2. Cassie will be more popular with her colleagues.
3. Conflict can be turned from a destructive force into a constructive force.
4. Cassie will be able to manage conflict rationally, not emotionally.
5. Cassie will see an immediate improvement in relationships in her workplace.

Answer:

By applying techniques to handle conflict better, Cassie will find that conflict can become a positive force--and that everyone can win. She will also find that she can handle conflict rationally, and not emotionally.

Option 1: This choice is correct. If Cassie applies techniques for better handling destructive conflict, she will see that conflict can be resolved to the satisfaction of all parties involved. In the end, everyone can benefit from these strategies.

Option 2: This is not correct. Cassie won't win any popularity contests by applying these techniques. In fact, she may become less popular. Cassie could upset the people who shy away from conflict as well as those who enjoy shouting matches.

Option 3: This option is correct. By applying techniques for handling destructive conflict better, Cassie will gain control of destructive impulses that may arise. From this position, she can deal with conflict in a productive and calm manner.

Option 4: This choice is correct. By applying these techniques, Cassie will learn to channel strong emotions that arise during conflict into a calm, rational mind-set that will help her deal effectively with conflict.

Option 5: Incorrect. Applying techniques to handle destructive conflict better will not necessarily lead to an overnight improvement in relationships at work. It is more likely that Cassie will see a long-term improvement in relationships.

Conflict will not dissipate of its own accord--someone has to make that happen. Using the techniques from this lesson, that person could be you.

How to confront conflict

Have you ever avoided conflict, or overreacted in a conflict situation? Although avoiding conflict or being competitive seem like sensible options, they are both problematic responses.

If you avoid conflict, you're only stockpiling trouble. Losing your temper is easy, and sometimes instinctive, but although you might initially overwhelm your colleagues, in the end they will look for revenge.

Question

Consider this situation.

You've had some alterations done to your house, and the final cost is twice the builder's initial estimate. The builder hasn't discussed the additional costs with you, or explained why he's gone over budget.

Options:

1. go for the builder's throat
2. shout and stomp around
3. say "that wasn't what you said"
4. pay up with gritted teeth
5. burst into tears

Answer:

Option 1: Reactions to conflict can range from aggression to avoidance, but neither are particularly effective. The middle ground between these extremes is confrontation, and used correctly it is an effective response to conflict.

Option 2: Reactions to conflict can range from aggression to avoidance, but neither are particularly effective. The middle ground between these extremes is confrontation, and used correctly it is an effective response to conflict.

Option 3: Reactions to conflict can range from aggression to avoidance, but neither are particularly effective. The middle ground between these extremes is confrontation, and used correctly it is an effective response to conflict.

Option 4: Reactions to conflict can range from aggression to avoidance, but neither are particularly effective. The middle ground between these extremes is confrontation, and used correctly it is an effective response to conflict.

Option 5: Reactions to conflict can range from aggression to avoidance, but neither are particularly effective. The middle ground between these extremes is confrontation, and used correctly it is an effective response to conflict.

First, it is important to define "confrontation," and explain how it differs from aggression and avoidance. Confrontation is an assertive response in which you calmly express your own view, and prepare for a mutual resolution.

See each behavior to get its definition.

Aggression

Aggression is when you verbally (or physically) attack and overwhelm the other

party so that you can achieve your goals.

Avoidance

Avoidance is when you totally give in to another point of view, even though you really don't agree with it.

Jenny, Helen, and Marsha are trying to work out how they will use a student intern in their department.

Jenny: Well, she's supporting me, and that's final. Don't try to convince me otherwise--I've made up my mind.

Helen: Oh...you two got most of the last intern's time, but if that's what you want, then I'll just have to deal with it.

Marsha: Hold on! I'm sure that we all need some support. I need some, and Helen is right to expect something from this intern, too. Why can't we share her?

In attempting to overwhelm the others, Jenny was being aggressive. Helen was acting against her real wishes to avoid the conflict, but Marsha gently confronted Jenny and proposed a win-win solution.

Question

Which statement correctly describes Marsha's confrontational approach to dealing with conflict?

Options:

1. Marsha attacked Jenny, and insisted that the intern would be shared between them.

2. Marsha calmly asserted herself, and proposed a mutual resolution.

3. Marsha didn't really agree with Jenny, but couldn't say so.

Answer:

Actually, Marsha's confrontational approach was calm and assertive, and she sought a mutually acceptable solution. She did not attack Jenny or avoid the issue by giving in.

Option 1: This does not accurately describe Marsha's confrontational approach. She did not use an aggressive approach in which she attacked Jenny to get her way. Further, she did not insist on her position; she proposed a different solution.

Option 2: This is an accurate description of Marsha's confrontational approach. Keeping her composure, she expressed her opinion and planned for a mutually beneficial solution. Marsha was assertive, not passive or aggressive.

Option 3: This is not an accurate description of the approach Marsha took. She did not totally give in to Jenny's point of view. If she had, she would have succumbed to Jenny's position that the intern be solely dedicated to her.

Confronting a colleague in a conflict situation can be daunting, as he or she may act aggressively. So you need to follow some guidelines about how to confront people properly. It's easy to become passive in the face of the other person's anger, or to get angry yourself.

But confrontational behavior involves different techniques, such as choosing the right context, having the right attitude, avoiding assumptions, and inviting a dialog.

See each element of confrontation to learn important guidelines that apply to these elements.

Context

The context in which you confront people is vitally important. You need to choose a time and a place that will not exacerbate the conflict, or make people act strangely to avoid losing face.

Attitude

Attitude is essential in confrontation. Whatever your real feelings, you need to show that you are in control, and express yourself firmly and clearly. If you are assertive, you send a calming message to the other person.

Assumptions

If you make assumptions about the other person, then you'll act on those assumptions--and often you'll be wrong. It is better to check the other party's real feelings and motives first.

Dialog

One of the defining parts of effective confrontation is dialog. You must act in a way that invites the other person to respond to you. Otherwise, you could end up either imposing an unacceptable solution, or reaching a stalemate.

In her dealings with Jenny and Helen, Marsha demonstrated that she is skilled in confronting conflict. Now review how she deals with Kevin.

Marsha: Kevin, can I speak to you? Is now a good time?

Kevin: Yes, now's OK. What do you want?

Marsha: It's about what you said to me at the staff meeting. I didn't feel that it was the right time or place to speak my mind, so I've left it until now. But I did not tell anyone that you were thinking of leaving, and I want you to acknowledge that. Your barbed comment really hurt me.

Kevin: Well, that's not what I heard.

Marsha: Kevin, I repeat, I did not say anything about you. I understand that someone else told you that I said that you had approached another company.

Kevin: Yes, Grace told me that.

Marsha: Why did you believe her, and not speak to me personally? Why make that hurtful statement in the meeting? I want to discuss this with you, and work out what we're going to do about it.

Question

Marsha did a great job of confronting Kevin.

Now match each of the four elements of effective confrontation with Marsha's actions. .

Options:

A. context
B. attitude
C. assumptions
D. dialog

Targets:

1. Marsha didn't try to anticipate Kevin's motives.
2. Marsha avoided approaching Kevin at an inappropriate time and place.
3. Marsha asked for Kevin's involvement in finding a solution.
4. Marsha was calmly assertive.

Answer:

Actually, Marsha avoided approaching Kevin in the meeting, waiting to find a suitable context. Her attitude was assertive, and she didn't make assumptions about Kevin's motives. She also invited Kevin into a dialog, to talk about the issue.

Marsha didn't make any faulty assumptions to add fuel to the fire. Instead, she checked with Kevin to hear his side of the story and to understand his motives before she jumped to conclusions.

Marsha made sure the context in which she confronted Kevin was appropriate. She could have confronted him during the meeting and caused him to lose face. Instead, she chose a time and place that wouldn't exacerbate the conflict.

When Marsha said she wanted to work out what they were going to do, she was inviting Kevin to have a dialog. She wanted his participation in finding an acceptable solution, not to impose a solution or reach a stalemate.

Marsha displayed the right attitude when confronting Kevin. Even though she was upset, she was in control and expressed herself firmly and clearly.

Marsha carefully considered all four elements of handling confrontation, and how to apply them to her particular circumstances.

See each element again to learn what else Marsha did to confront appropriately.

Context

Marsha avoided a public place, and she also used neutral territory, so that no one had an advantage. Kevin volunteered that he had enough time for the discussion, so she knew that the issue could be resolved immediately.

Attitude

Marsha was firm, but not threatening. She described the problem and how it made her feel, before she stated clearly what she wanted out of the discussion with Kevin.

Assumptions

Marsha wanted Kevin to explain his motives. But she avoided responding to him as though she knew what he was feeling already, or what he was trying to achieve. She avoided being judgmental.

Dialog

Marsha attempted to open a dialog with Kevin. To do this, she actively listened to him, and then she responded in order to engage him in a discussion. This showed her intention to work towards a compromise.

When you confronted him without assumptions, it left the space for him to enter into a dialog with you. Only by asking for his input could you reach a mutually acceptable solution.

Case Study: Question 1 of 3

Scenario

For your convenience, the case study is repeated with each question.

Estelle is one of your colleagues, and you have to work closely with her to meet your weekly sales target.

For the last few days, Estelle has not been working as hard as usual. As a result, both of you have had to work late to meet your target.

You decide that you are going to confront Estelle about the problem.

Answer the questions, in order, to show how you will confront Estelle most effectively.

Question

You are having lunch in the cafeteria with Estelle and some other colleagues, when Estelle says that she is sick of having to work late. What should you say to her?
Options:
1. "Actually, the trouble is that you're not contributing your fair share of the workload."
2. "Yes, that's a problem for me as well. Why don't we talk about it back at the office today?"
3. "Estelle, why aren't you working as hard as you used to?"

Answer:
Talking about this in a public place in front of other people will make Estelle behave defensively. For effective confrontation, speak to her in a private, neutral place.

Option 1: This option is not correct. By confronting Estelle in the cafeteria in front of other colleagues, you are forgetting to prioritize the context. Estelle will lose face in this setting and is likely to react defensively.

Option 2: This approach is a good one because you have broached the topic with Estelle but have proposed discussing it at a time and place that will not exacerbate the conflict and result in her losing face.

Option 3: This choice is not correct. Although you frame the issue clearly for Estelle, you have not chosen the right time or place for a confrontation. Confronting Estelle in a public setting in front of colleagues is not an effective strategy.

Case Study: Question 2 of 3
You meet up with Estelle in a meeting room. Which statements would be most appropriate in order to continue the confrontation?
Options:

1. "Estelle, the problem is that I don't feel that you are working as hard as you used to."

2. "What's up with you? You're acting so weird lately."

3. "I know that you're ashamed about the fact that you aren't working as hard as I am, but we need to talk about it."

4. "You said that you were sick of working late. What do you think the problem is?"

5. "Estelle, there seem to be some problems with our sales targets."

Answer:

Confrontation is most effective when the problem is clearly stated, and you do not make assumptions about how the other party sees the problem. Being ambiguous or judgmental will get you nowhere.

Option 1: This choice is correct because it is a clear statement of the problem and how you feel about it. You are acting with a firm and assertive attitude.

Option 2: This is not correct. It reveals your judgmental attitude toward Estelle. This judgmental approach will only alienate her and take you further away from a workable solution.

Option 3: This is incorrect. This statement reveals an unconfirmed assumption on your part: that Estelle is ashamed because you are working harder. It's important to avoid making assumptions if the confrontation is to be successful.

Option 4: This is an effective approach to use with Estelle. You are checking with her to understand her perspective and avoid making assumptions or jumping to conclusions. This will help you move forward with your confrontation.

Option 5: This is not the most effective approach because you are not clearly stating the problem. This is an indirect way of saying that Estelle is not pulling her weight. If you use this approach, Estelle won't understand what the problem is.

Case Study: Question 3 of 3

Estelle now says that you are unfairly blaming her. How should you respond?

Options:

1. "Well, what's the best way to get you moving again?"
2. "Tell me why you think that I've been unfair."
3. "Well, I'm not going to listen to you trying to blame me!"
4. "So, what do you think would be the best solution?"

Answer:

Actually, the way to progress is to set up a dialog with Estelle, listening to her and seeking her views, to reach a mutually agreeable solution.

Option 1: This option is not correct. Although this question may initiate a dialog with Estelle, it will continue to make her feel judged and attacked. You are closing a door and not moving any closer to a resolution.

Option 2: This choice is correct because you are acting in a way that invites Estelle to respond to you. You are initiating a dialog, which will help you reach a mutually beneficial solution.

Option 3: This option is not correct. Getting defensive with Estelle will alienate her so she won't be willing to reach a compromise of any kind.

Option 4: This choice is correct because asking for Estelle's input on the matter opens up a dialog with her. This will help you reach a compromise.

Confronting conflict takes skill and sensitivity. Using these techniques to deal with conflict calmly and fairly makes it much more likely that you'll reach a conclusion which benefits both parties.

Communication and conflict

When groups or individuals fail to communicate, they often find themselves in conflict. And when they are in conflict, they often fail to communicate. So communication problems are both the cause and the result of conflict in the workplace.

Therefore, communication skills are a vital element of your conflict handling repertoire.

Communication is concerned with understanding other points of view. If you can't see things from someone else's viewpoint, then your positions become more and more polarized.

The gap between your perceptions and the other person's perceptions grows larger and larger, and becomes harder and harder to bridge.

Elroy, Andy, Jess, and Nick have all experienced conflict in the workplace.

See each person to learn about their experiences with polarized communication.

Elroy

Elroy was ostracized by his colleagues after he criticized Mary for being upset about her dog's death. Elroy didn't realize how close Mary was to her dog. This knowledge gap made him appear rude, and things got worse from there.

Andy

Each day, Andy was supposed to get Conrad to check his work. But instead, he waited until he had a large volume, and then handed it over. He was surprised when Conrad got really annoyed.

Jess

When Jess was rushing, she'd use any parking space, and didn't mind if somebody used hers. After arriving late one day and parking in someone else's spot, she returned to find an irate note on her car. Then she knew how annoyed people were by this.

Nick

Six months after he refused to swap shifts with Katy to accommodate her childcare arrangements, Nick was transferred to her department. He was ostracized, and Katy nearly lost her job over the issue. No one will associate with Nick now.

Elroy, Andy, Jess, and Nick, and their colleagues, failed to communicate, and this led to escalating conflict.

- Elroy didn't appreciate how insensitive he appeared to be.
- Andy failed to understand things from Conrad's point of view.
- Jess couldn't see that others were annoyed by her parking.
- Nick didn't realize how bad things were with Katy until it was too late.

So what could these people do to improve their communication skills?

They need to consider three essential techniques that will make their communication much more effective in conflict situations.

Check each technique in turn for more information about how each technique can improve communication.

Linkages

Ideas should be linked to people so that they are not abstract concepts. Put a face to the issue and you will be more sensitive about how you approach it. If Andy had linked his behavior to Conrad, he would have been more thoughtful.

Significance

Establish the significance of issues. People's issues are important to them, and ignoring them can have major implications. Elroy didn't see the significance of Mary's dog's death, and Jess ignored the effect that her parking had on others.

Intentions

You need to make your cooperative intentions clear. Listening is good, but an explicit statement about compromise goes further. Nick should have shown such intentions towards Katy.

Elroy and the others have learned from their experiences, and so when faced with other potential conflict situations, they try to implement the techniques.

Elroy: I'm supposed to follow some really dumb regulations about using the computer. Usually I would just ignore them, but this time I found out who had suggested them, went to see her, and talked it through. I still think that they're too involved, but Claire and I modified them a little, and she was nice.

Andy: Now that I'm a manager, I have to keep sickness records for my team. I wasn't going to, but I decided to speak to the clerk involved. He explained what would happen if I didn't keep accurate records. To be honest, I hadn't appreciated the consequences of my actions.

Jess: When Cindy joined our office, I showed her the ropes. She asked about who looked after the telephones during lunch, and I told her that we all took turns, but that if she had any problems, she could swap with me. Someone overheard our discussion, and we all agreed to apply a similar system throughout the office.

Nick: I've joined a new division. It's hard to get lab time, but I've noticed that everyone works together if they have a real crisis. Someone always manages to move their lab sessions around to accommodate others. People even manage to joke about it.

Elroy found out who was responsible for the computer regulations, and making a linkage between ideas and a person helped him to manage his conflict with Claire effectively. Jess and Nick found the value of expressing clear cooperative intentions.

Andy was successful because he found that knowing how important an idea is to someone could help him to manage his conflict with another person. Communication is a vital tool in dealing with conflict with others.

According to research about communication and conflict, the amount of communication between groups has a significant effect on the likelihood of conflict. The potential for conflict increases if there is too much or too little communication between groups. It is therefore possible to "over communicate" as well as "under communicate." So the techniques for creating more effective communication must not be used indiscriminately. They have to be carefully applied.

Question

When Jack introduced communication training to improve conflict management, a lot of people were skeptical. Jack explained that effective conflict communication was underpinned by three main aspects: linkages, significance, and intentions. Which of Jack's statements correctly describe these aspects?

Options:

1. "Linkage means attaching ideas to people so that they aren't abstract concepts."

2. "Significance means not ignoring people's issues--they're important to them."

3. "It's important to attach a face to an issue. This is what I mean by significance."

4. "As part of demonstrating your intentions, you should understand how someone feels."

5. "Showing intentions means listening and stating that you're willing to compromise."

Answer:

Linkages are about attaching ideas to people, whereas significance means understanding what an issue means to someone. You should also explicitly show your intent to reach a solution.

Option 1: This statement correctly describes the aspect of linkages. It is easier to neglect a work issue or policy if it is just an abstract concept. But as soon as a person is associated with the issue or policy, it is easier to see that sensitivity is required.

Option 2: This is correct. This statement addresses the importance of significance. It's important to acknowledge people's issues. Minimizing or ignoring them can have major implications.

Option 3: This option is not correct because attaching a face to an issue is called linkage, not significance. Significance is acknowledging the importance of someone else's issue even if it seems insignificant to an outside observer.

Option 4: This choice is not correct. Grasping how someone else feels is not the purpose of demonstrating intentions. Understanding someone else's feelings doesn't go far enough in demonstrating your intention to compromise.

Option 5: This option is correct. This correctly describes the aspect of showing intentions. The purpose of this aspect is to make clear one's intention to cooperate or reach a mutually agreed-on solution with the other party.

To apply these techniques in the workplace, you need to go beyond the level of individual skills and move towards organization-wide efforts, implemented at the managerial level. This shift in emphasis requires a translation of these simple techniques into organizational procedures that will improve communication.

Read about each technique to find out how it can be applied across an organization.

linking ideas to people

Create cross-functional teams in which people work with a range of colleagues. Interactions will then lead to a wider recognition of individuals and their qualities. This technique is particularly useful in resolving role conflict based on different technical or professional backgrounds.

identifying the significance of issues

Organize a regular pattern of secondment--temporary transfer--between departments and functions. This will enable people to experience things from different perspectives. This is a useful technique for workers with a history of embedded conflict where the expectations of coworkers are fixed.

encouraging cooperative intent

Give certain individuals the specific job of coordinating understanding between departments. These people should be proactive individuals who will speed up communication by taking charge and energizing the process. Do not make this role too complex, and it will have an immediate impact.

Good communication does not depend on good fortune. Be proactive about improving communication and cooperation, because while clashing needs cause conflict, shared goals make people work together.

Determining an Acceptable Outcome

Imagine that you're racing for the only available parking space when somebody cuts in front of you and parks. You have an argument about it, neither person listening to or caring about the other's feelings. So what's the difference between this scenario and conflict at work?

The difference is that you'll probably never see that stranger again, but you have to continue working with your colleagues. Ongoing relationships affect the outcome of arguments.

What you should be aiming for is an outcome that is satisfactory to both of you, but which doesn't surrender too many of your interests for the sake of the relationship. The way to achieve this is to use an integrative bargaining style instead of a distributive bargaining style.

See each bargaining style for an explanation.

Distributive bargaining

This is based on the assumption that the outcome is fixed, so that if you gain, someone else must lose. It is often referred to as competitive bargaining.

Integrative bargaining

This is based upon the assumption that, through compromise, both sides can achieve some outcome, and the intention is to maximize both outcome.

Jeremy, Anne, Alistair, and Maisie are identifying some simple integrative and distributive bargaining approaches and their outcomes.

Read about each person to reveal their tactic.

Jeremy

Jeremy told his co-worker Elly that he had decided how to allocate their duties. Elly suggested that they discuss incoming projects to see which person suited which task best, but Jeremy refused. He said that as he was senior, he should decide.

Alistair

Alistair asked his team to make proposals about spending the software budget, but then he bought the planning software that was relevant to his job, but not to his team members' jobs. He told them that there wasn't enough money to meet all of their software requests.

Anne

Tim wanted to work extra hours, and Anne wanted to work part-time while her children were young. Anne proposed to her boss that if she cut her hours for three years, Tim could do them, but after that, she wanted to revert to full-time again.

Maisie

Maisie declined the new corner office because, as she was out of the building so often, it would usually be empty. She proposed that Jim use it, if he agreed to letting her use it when she needed to meet an important client.

Alistair and Jeremy are clearly using competitive approaches. They took all, and gave nothing away. But Anne and Maisie found compromises that suited everybody without surrendering their own needs and interests.

Question

Aleesha and Amy are colleagues and team leaders, but they work very differently. One of them takes an integrative approach to negotiations within her team, whereas the other follows distributive bargaining principles. Consider their comments, and then select the person who takes an integrative approach.

Options:

1. Aleesha says: "I feel like the pot only has so much in it, so I encourage my people to compete--and the winner takes all."

2. Amy says: "I feel that the team gains more if everybody gets in on the action. So I encourage them to share things around."

Answer:

Amy employs an integrative approach, trying to manage through compromise and sharing of resources. Aleesha's philosophy is one of distributive bargaining--if one person wins, then another loses.

Option 1: Aleesha's approach is a distributive one, not an integrative one. Her approach is based on the assumption that the outcome is fixed so that if one person gains, someone else must lose.

Option 2: Amy takes an integrative approach with her team. This approach is based on the belief that, through collaboration and compromise, both sides can achieve some outcome, and the intention is to maximize both outcomes.

The integrative approach is based upon the attitude that the best outcome of any conflict is when everybody gains something.

You need to follow three steps to achieve an outcome that is acceptable to all.

See each step in turn, starting with planning, for more information on integrative bargaining.

Planning

First, you need to establish the minimal acceptable outcome for you, and then imagine what would be in it for the other person. In planning, you decide what you must have, and what you are willing to trade.

Negotiation

In the actual negotiation, you need to adopt a rational approach. Conflict is inevitably emotional, but this is rarely helpful. Use rational problem-solving techniques to safely move you from argument to counter argument.

Outcomes

If you want to make the integrative approach work, you need to establish tangible outcomes. These outcomes must benefit both parties directly.

Anne and Maisie use these techniques in their own negotiations to achieve outcomes that are acceptable to all.

Anne: I've found that preparation pays off. I always take the time to work out the best possible compromise. I start from the least that I'm willing to accept. That's my baseline, and I work up from that.

Maisie: That's simple, compared to working out the other side's baseline! But if you really try to put yourself in their shoes, you can usually do it.

Anne: I also propose compromises quickly. I've found that the more direct you are, the better. I used to play a lot of games, pretending to offer something lower than I thought they would accept. But now, I take all the emotion and drama out of it.

Maisie: I agree. It's important to be clear and rational, and to suggest compromises that will work. I hate those situations where it sounds good, but on closer inspection you're not gaining much.

Question

Anne and Maisie are applying the three steps to achieve an acceptable resolution, but what are they actually doing? Match each step with its description.

Options:

A. planning
B. negotiation
C. outcomes

Targets:

1. problem-solving using a rational approach
2. deciding what you want, and what you're willing to trade
3. determining tangible results that will benefit both parties

Answer:

First, you need to plan what you are prepared to offer and accept. Second, you need to negotiate using rational arguments. Finally, you should create outcomes that benefit both parties.

This describes the negotiation step during which you must adopt a rational approach. Use rational problem-solving techniques to safely move you from argument to counter argument.

This describes the planning step. During this step, you must establish the minimal acceptable outcome for you and imagine what would be in it for the other person. You decide what you must have and what you are willing to trade.

This describes the outcomes step. To make the integrative approach work, you must establish tangible outcomes that benefit both parties directly.

Alistair and Jeremy are discovering that their competitive approaches aren't successful. Most people respond by being as uncompromising as Alistair and Jeremy are, leading to stalemates.

They recognize that Maisie has a better way to deal with disputes, and ask her to explain her approach.

See each step of integrative bargaining to reveal what Maisie tells them.

planning

"You need to distinguish between what you want and what you will accept. There's often a difference, which gives you flexibility. The other person will have their own range of wants. Try to identify their interests--what lies behind the position that they take?"

negotiation

"Avoid becoming emotional. I'm not saying not to care, but don't personalize the issues. The hardest thing for you will be when you're challenged. Then you need to concentrate on what people are saying, not how they are saying it."

outcomes

"You've got to work on outcomes that aren't just platitudes. It's easy to agree to something, but then do nothing. I make sure that whatever we agree to is measurable, and includes a deadline. That way we end up with real benefits."

Alistair and Jeremy are still uncertain about Maisie's approach, so they visit Anne to see if she can reassure them.

Anne: I know that it's hard to change your behavior, but believe me, integrative bargaining works.

Jeremy: Give us an example of how you've used it.

Anne: OK. I had to review and revise the web site last month. Tig wasn't happy about it, as he did it the last time. I knew that I had to meet with him, so that he could tell me about the design. That's where planning came in.

Alistair: How did you plan the meeting?

Anne: First, I thought about my position. I'm happy to review the content, but less confident about the design, particularly if the issues are technical. Tig, on the other hand, is a "techie" and that's how he wants to make his mark. So it was easy to reach a compromise.

Alistair: No way! Nothing is easy with Tig. We nearly had a fight the last time that we disagreed with each other.

Anne: Well, he was aggressive. But I kept calm, and focused on the issues. He shouted, but each time I responded to a point, he calmed down. In the end, we agreed that I'd do the review, then give him a report, and he'd fix the technical issues. It was a perfect compromise.

Jeremy: I see. So you get credit for the review, and he gets credit for the revisions. Everybody is satisfied, and your relationship with Tig improves. Well, we can certainly learn from that.

In the following scenario, try to resolve a dispute with Don to your mutual satisfaction. But first, select each element to remind yourself about how Maisie and Anne behaved.

Plan

Anne and Maisie worked hard at their planning. Anne sorted out in her mind that her target was the review, and that she didn't want to do the redesign. She then put herself into Tig's shoes and saw that what he would want made a compromise possible.

Keep calm

Anne and Maisie stressed the need to keep calm and unemotional. Anne was certainly provoked by Tig's shouting, but she responded by returning to the issue each time. This in the end returned the focus to the discussion and led to the agreement.

Negotiate and outcome

Anne and Maisie agreed to concrete outcomes. Anne negotiated with Tig, agreeing that she would review the content and he would review the technical aspects. This is the sort of result you should be aiming for, one that will really affect future projects.

If you want to be successful in handling conflict with others, then don't forget how to plan the discussion, and conduct yourself rationally to produce an outcome that gives tangible benefits to all.

Surviving Conflict

How many times has someone said to you: "Well, whose side are you on?" during an argument between two warring parties. But this isn't an invitation--it's a threat.

Taking sides in someone else's conflict is risky. At the very least, you'll upset one party. But if you try to avoid taking sides at all, you could alienate both parties.

When people argue, and you are a bystander, it's tempting to wade in and act as a mediator to calm things down. But beware--the person in the middle often gets hurt the most.

In many workplaces, mediation is an official role. A mediator has the power to insist upon a compromise. But placing yourself in the middle of warring colleagues is different. It involves acting as an unofficial mediator.

What's the best way to prevent a fire from growing?
- Throw more fuel on it?
- Stop putting fuel on it?

The answer is, of course, obvious. The only way to stop a fire from growing is to stop feeding it. Without fuel it dies away, and the same applies to conflict.

Techniques used to survive conflict

At her exit interview, Connie gave some short and sharp answers to her interviewer. No, she had not gained from the experience, and yes, she knew what the problem was.

In her words, she was surrounded by "weaklings and backstabbers." The company was full of people fighting each other, and it affected her so much that it was time to leave.

Managing Workplace Conflicts

Connie was surrounded by conflict, and found it difficult to avoid being involved. She was sometimes an ally, sometimes a victim, but hardly ever an innocent bystander.

There are three ways to deal with conflict when you are surrounded by it. Connie tried the first two, but not the third, and that's why she left. The three approaches are:
- taking sides,
- mediating,
- remaining separate.

Connie is much happier in her new job--not because the feuding doesn't occur, but because she's learned new approaches and techniques for surviving them.

Connie: Now I know how to keep away from conflict, and still cultivate good working relationships. I've found that I can deal with it, and keep my professional reputation intact. It's true--there's a stress-free way to survive conflict.

For Connie, the workplace is now a pleasant and comfortable environment. And she knows why things are better. She's realized that she can use techniques to survive conflict, and therefore benefit by:
- sustaining good working relationships,
- maintaining a professional image,
- accomplishing her work with minimal stress.

But Connie hasn't avoided all conflicts. A couple of times, her loyalty and principles made her join a conflict situation. Once or twice, she even made a provocative comment just for the fun of it. But she knows now how to control her involvement, and what the consequences are if she doesn't.

Question

Disputes and arguments are also common in Rob's team. He hates the atmosphere, and wants to find a way to survive when surrounded by conflict. What benefits would Rob realize by learning conflict survival techniques?

Options:

1. He could still provoke people and get away with it.
2. He could maintain a professional image.
3. He could learn how to manage his principles better.
4. He could learn how to sustain good working relationships.
5. His work would become less stressful.

Answer:

Surviving conflict doesn't mean that you sacrifice your professional image or working relationships--you can enhance both. And conflict survival techniques will make your working life less stressful.

Option 1: This choice is not correct. The point of learning conflict survival techniques is not to play games with people and get away with it.

Option 2: This is a correct choice. Rob can enhance his professional image by learning conflict survival techniques. If he uses these techniques to stay neutral and objective, he will be seen as professional and level-headed.

Option 3: This option is not correct. Learning conflict survival techniques will not necessarily help Rob better manage his principles. Managing principles is a reflective, solitary process, not a conflict survival strategy.

Option 4: This option is correct. By learning conflict survival strategies, Rob can avoid taking sides and alienating co-workers. He can also prevent being caught in the cross fire. That way, he can maintain positive working relationships with his colleagues.

Option 5: This choice is correct. By learning conflict survival techniques, Rob can avoid taking sides or acting as a mediator in disputes and decrease his stress level at work.

To avoid a situation like Connie's, make sure that you use the techniques in this lesson to survive endemic conflict. By using these techniques, not only will you be less stressed, but you can also enhance your relationships and reputation.

Avoiding taking sides

How many times has someone said to you: "Well, whose side are you on?" during an argument between two warring parties. But this isn't an invitation--it's a threat.

Taking sides in someone else's conflict is risky. At the very least, you'll upset one party. But if you try to avoid taking sides at all, you could alienate both parties.

Workplace conflict can be destructive. Disputes can stem from small incidents, distracting people from important issues. When conflict is the norm rather than the exception, you can be pulled into countless pointless arguments that sap your energy. If this sounds like your organization, you want a way to survive conflict with the least discomfort. One way is to avoid taking sides.

Not taking sides sounds like a simple approach, although it can be difficult initially. But even if it is difficult, it's better than being drawn into fruitless arguments. Like Stacey and Alistair, you can do one of two things.

See each person to learn how they avoided taking sides.

Alistair

"You just refuse to comment. It sounds easy, but in fact it's pretty hard to do sometimes."

Stacey

"I've found that if you take a lot of time to consider both arguments, people accept that and things calm down. I pride myself on thinking before speaking."

Stacey and Alistair found that by avoiding taking sides in disputes, their working life improved.

Alistair: My approach hasn't always made me popular. At first, I used to get a lot of flak about it, but now more and more people are coming around to my way of thinking. If a couple of guys want to have an argument, that's their business, but I won't get involved. If I have an argument, I expect everybody else to stay away.

Stacey: I suppose that because I am cautious, it's easier for me. I don't yell at people, I stop and think about what I really feel. Nine times out of ten, it all blows over. That's how I keep from being dragged into things.

For many people, outright refusal or prevarication contradicts their instincts. Arguments are like whirlpools--they pull you in, and some people offer less resistance than others. Arguments can also be stimulating and invigorating, which is attractive to some people. But when conflicts are continuous, instead of being energizing they can drain energy. This is when not taking sides becomes a more sensible option.

Question

What are the methods that Alistair and Stacey use to avoid taking sides in conflicts at work?

Options:

1. refusing to take part

2. stimulating discussion
3. fostering the spirit of debate
4. considering arguments in detail
Answer:

In fact, refusal and detailed consideration are the methods to use if you want to avoid taking sides in a conflict.

Option 1: This choice is correct. Although you may feel pressure to participate, if you want to avoid taking sides in a conflict, you should refrain from commenting. You can do so politely so you don't alienate either party.

Option 2: This option is not correct. By stimulating discussion, you can get caught up in a conflict. And before you know it, you may be perceived as siding with one party or another.

Option 3: This choice is incorrect because encouraging debate doesn't make you a neutral bystander. By doing this, you might get pulled into the conflict.

Option 4: This option is correct. Taking time to consider both sides allows you to remain neutral and not get pulled into the fray.

So, to avoid taking sides, either simply refuse to take part in the conflict, or consider the arguments for so long that the conflict dies out, or is resolved before you have to commit to either side. Both of these approaches need to be carefully handled so as not to alienate your warring colleagues. You need to leave them feeling positive--or at worst, neutral--about you.

See each method to find out how to avoid taking sides and achieve a positive outcome.

Refuse

If you make your statement of refusal politely, then you can minimize any negative reactions. You must phrase it so that both parties understand that it applies to both of them equally.

Consider the arguments

Saying that you'll consider the arguments carefully is, in essence, evading the decision. You must emphasize that you're thinking deeply about the merits of each point of view, and that this could take you a long time.

By refusing or prevaricating, Alistair and Stacey have found out exactly how to keep their colleagues positive. Reveal how they handle their chosen approaches to conflict.

Alistair: I listen to what they say, so that no one thinks that I'm being rude. Then I politely refuse to get involved. Sometimes I have to repeat this, and people do get annoyed. But I just stay calm, and I make sure that they know that I've said the same thing to the other side.

Stacey: You can't just ignore what people say. They can get passionate, so I try to understand what they mean. I summarize their arguments, and go back over each point to make sure that I've got it. I'm not acting--I really want to understand the full story.

Question

Tim is uncomfortable in his turbulent workplace. In the future, he wants to avoid taking sides in the constant disputes that erupt every day. Which statements explain how to do this?

Options:

1. Politeness reduces the impact of refusal.
2. Explain that you must carefully consider the merits of each argument.

3. Tell the combatants that it takes times to understand complex arguments.

4. It's important to hear each argument more than once.

5. Both sides must be aware that your stance applies to them both.

Answer:

Actually, politeness and equality are the essential elements of refusal. For prevarication, you must explain how carefully you need to consider each argument, and that this takes time.

Option 1: This option is correct. By politely refusing to take part in the conflict, Tim can minimize any negative reactions. This will ensure that he doesn't alienate either party.

Option 2: This choice is correct. By explaining that he needs time to consider the arguments carefully, Tim is evading the decision and staying out of the conflict.

Option 3: This is correct. Tim can avoid taking sides by emphasizing that he is thinking deeply about the merits of each point of view and that this could take a long time. This buys him time and helps him avoid involvement in the conflict.

Option 4: This option is not correct. This action would increase Tim's involvement in the conflict. Both parties would attempt to persuade him to align with their argument.

Option 5: This is a correct choice. If Tim makes his statement of refusal and emphasizes that it applies to both parties, he will underscore his neutrality and avoid getting pulled into the conflict.

If done badly, refusal or prevarication can be damaging to work relationships. See each technique to discover how to apply it effectively.

Refuse

Do not refuse to get involved without giving a reason. Your reason could be that both arguments have equal merit, or conversely that neither argument is justifiable. You can also cite a lack of knowledge of the issue.

Prevaricate

This involves lengthy questioning of both sides to establish the arguments. Conflict often leads to emotional appeals, so an effective technique is to focus on the facts of the arguments, not the feelings.

Case Study: Question 1 of 2

Scenario

You are a member of a small team. Terry is arguing with Dave, another team member, about how long the project that you're all working on will take. Terry and Dave both want you to get involved in the argument, but you've had enough of their constant arguing, which they seem to enjoy, but which you find distracting.

Demonstrate how to avoid taking sides in this conflict by answering the questions, in order.

Question:

Terry argues that the schedule for the project needs to include three days for unforeseeable delays. Dave argues that two days are enough. Terry asks you to support him. How should you reply?

Options:

1. "Terry, I haven't got time for this now. Don't try to pull me into your dumb arguments."

2. "Both of you are just guessing--you can't predict the unpredictable. So I really can't say either way."

3. "Over a four-month project, it really doesn't make much difference whether we allow two or three days. So I'm happy to stay out of it--sorry!"

4. "Well, I don't know how many days we need. OK, I'll go with Terry's argument."

Answer:

Actually, you should have chosen responses which point out that both arguments are equally weak. You also need to be polite!

Option 1: This choice is not correct. Although you are clearly stating your desire to stay out of the conflict, you did so in an impolite manner. Insulting Terry and Dave is not an effective strategy and may increase hostilities.

Option 2: This choice is correct. You are pointing out the fact that no one really knows enough to make an informed decision. Your response is clear and states that arguing without proper knowledge is pointless.

Option 3: This is correct. Clearly pointing out a lack of knowledge about this scheduling issue is an effective avoidance strategy. You've indicated that both arguments are equally weak and made it clear that you're not showing any favoritism.

Option 4: This choice is not correct. You have just taken sides, even though you admit that you don't know how many days are needed.

Case Study: Question 2 of 2

Dave wants the team to work on the project simultaneously with another one, but Terry thinks that they should run sequentially. Dave loses his temper, and demands that you support him because he always supports you. He says that if you don't, he won't speak to you again! How should you reply to him, in order to prevaricate?

Options:

1. "Dave, tell me why the projects should run together. And how we will do them both at the same time."

2. "Dave, calm down. Yelling at me won't help me to see what you're talking about. Now, explain it to me carefully."

3. "Take back what you said, or I'm not talking to you, either."

4. "Dave, I don't think that this is important enough for me to get involved. You'd better leave me out of it."

Answer:

In fact, by asking Dave questions, and keeping emotions out of it, you can show that you're going to consider the facts only, in great depth. Giving this issue serious consideration will help you to delay taking sides.

Option 1: This option is correct. By posing questions, you demonstrate that you're giving careful consideration to the arguments, which delays your involvement.

Option 2: This choice is correct. You are showing that you will not permit emotions to overrule intellect. Repetition of this message is an effective tactic.

Option 3: This is not correct. You have been pulled into the fray by Dave's emotional appeal and are now reacting to his threat. This will not help you stay neutral.

Option 4: This is not correct because by responding in this way, you are not prevaricating. You are refusing to take sides.

Remaining neutral isn't always easy, as work colleagues can be very demanding of your support. But these techniques will help you to delay taking sides, hopefully until the conflict fades away by itself.

Avoiding being caught in the middle

When people argue, and you are a bystander, it's tempting to wade in and act as a mediator to calm things down. But beware--the person in the middle often gets hurt the most.

In many workplaces, mediation is an official role. A mediator has the power to insist upon a compromise. But placing yourself in the middle of warring colleagues is different. It involves acting as an unofficial mediator.

Unofficial mediators try to find the middle ground between two parties, and encourage them to communicate and reach a resolution themselves.

However, unofficial mediators are powerless. You have no powers to bring the sides together, or to insist upon a compromise. And if you fail, the blame for the entire dispute will often fall on you.

There are good reasons for not being caught in the middle of two fighting parties. But sometimes your colleagues can be very persuasive, calling on your loyalties or friendships. So you need to develop ways to avoid the situation.

See each of these three effective techniques to learn more about avoiding conflict.

refer them to another party

Refer the conflict to an official mediator in the organization. This will usually be someone who has the authority to enforce a solution.

choose a side

Review the arguments, and declare your interests. However, then you cannot mediate. This will, of course, bring its own set of problems. But in certain instances, for example, when the argument is trivial, it is a less dangerous course of action.

use reasoning

Offer a rational and detailed analysis of the problem, and emphasize the distance between the two sides. The longer and more pessimistic the analysis, the better, since a negative approach shows that you can't provide a way forward.

Now follow Larry, Kim, and Hazel as they describe how they have avoided getting caught in the middle.

Larry: Carlos and Roy are not easy to work with. They don't get along, and I used to try to work out their issues. But I could never get them to agree with each other. Now I don't bother. If they fight, I just tell them to take it to the boss. He can work it out. They have to listen to him.

Kim: Jeanie and Nessie argue all of the time, about the most trivial things. I quickly review each argument and declare which one I support--they're usually almost the same! That way I don't get stuck in the middle.

Hazel: Well, I've found that if you look at the gap between the two sides, and emphasize the distance between them, people don't want you to get involved. If they want a mediator, they are looking for a solution, and if you tell them that you can't see one, they don't want you. It's as simple as that!

Question

Larry, Kim, and Hazel described three ways to avoid being caught in the middle of other people's arguments.

Match each technique with the appropriate comment.
Options:
A. use reasoning
B. choose a side
C. refer to another party
Targets:
1. "Review the arguments, decide which one you agree with, and stick to that view."
2. "Analyze each side of the argument, and explain the flaws in each."
3. "Recommend that they talk to someone in authority."
Answer:
Using reasoning involves looking at the arguments and emphasizing the distance between the two sides. You could also review the arguments and choose a side, or refer the argument to someone who has real authority.

This is an example of choosing a side. By aligning with one person in the conflict, you are well positioned to mediate.

This is an example of using reasoning. If you present a detailed analysis of the problem in a pessimistic light, your negative approach will demonstrate that you can't provide a way forward.

This is an example of referring the people in conflict to another party. You should refer them to someone who is an official mediator in the organization and who has the authority to enforce a solution.

Trying to avoid acting as an unofficial mediator is a delicate operation. You must first engage with the parties to inform them or convince them that you are not going to take on the role, and then withdraw. You must handle this engagement sensitively, to prevent it escalating into anger or blame.

See each technique to find out more.

Refer upwards

To pass the argument on to an official mediator, convince the warring parties that they need to involve someone who can enforce a decision--that you will be able to do little for them. Always explain what you're going to do, and why.

Choose a side

Declaring an interest in the argument is risky, so do it early in the process. You use this tactic for trivial arguments, but you should explain that you have a reason for your choice--perhaps one idea has slightly more merit.

Use reason

Detailing the merits of each argument is close to acting as an unofficial mediator, so don't encourage the parties to explain their arguments. Instead, focus on the fact that the sides are so far apart that you can't solve the problem.

Larry, Kim, and Hazel have already outlined how they avoided acting as unofficial mediators. They applied the techniques of choosing a side, referring the dispute upwards, or using reasoning.

Now review what they say about how they engaged and then withdrew from disputes.

Hazel: Neil and Susan had their most bitter arguments when I was around, and they'd say "What do you think, Hazel?" Now they wouldn't dream of asking me to get involved. The last time they argued about where to go for lunch, I listed every restaurant we'd been to and commented on them. It took twenty minutes.

Kim: I do that, too. People don't really want to listen to what you're saying. They want to be the center of attention. When the team argued about bonuses, I pointed out that the difference between sales and secretarial bonuses was over 40 per cent, so there was no point talking about it. Nobody tried to get me to mediate after that.

Larry: And have you noticed that if you get in really quickly and tell people that you favor one side, they leave you alone? That's how I handle Neil and Susan. Susan is my friend, but I've even done it to her by telling her that the other side has a better argument.

Kim: The last time that Neil and Susan tried to get me involved, I just told Kirstie about it. She's their boss, so it should be her concern. They didn't thank me, though, when she told them to stop squabbling and get back to work.

Hazel: Leroy and Estelle are more reasonable. They knew that they'd never agree with each other, so when I suggested that Vincent make the decision, they were happy. He was allocating the funds anyway, so it made sense.

Remember that referral needs to be handled sensitively. Don't just go over the heads of your colleagues. Ask the advice of the authority figure, but don't force the issue.

No matter how well you handle it, declining to act as a mediator may make you unpopular at times. Dealing with conflict is never easy, but at least you'll gain your colleagues' respect, even if you don't give them what they want.

Changing the atmosphere

What's the best way to prevent a fire from growing?
- Throw more fuel on it?
- Stop putting fuel on it?

The answer is, of course, obvious. The only way to stop a fire from growing is to stop feeding it. Without fuel it dies away, and the same applies to conflict.

Simple differences of opinion can be fueled and fanned into flame by the workplace atmosphere, until they flare up in raging conflicts. So you have to create an atmosphere that does not feed conflict.

Nat and Emily compare the attitudes to conflict in their respective organizations.

Emily: Most people here seem to think that the constant fighting is not their problem. If they aren't directly involved, then they believe that how they behave otherwise isn't important.

Nat: Our workplace was like that--only fun if you liked constant fighting. But we started to see that we encouraged pointless conflict. So we stopped, and decided on an unofficial code of conduct. The place has been transformed.

Emily: So you don't have any conflict?

Nat: No, we still have plenty of healthy disagreements. What we don't have are dumb arguments over petty issues that somehow end up engulfing us all.

Emily: How did you achieve that?

Nat: The key for us was personal behavior. We decided that if everybody acted professionally with their colleagues, then the source and energy for most of the unnecessary conflicts would be removed. And it worked.

Introducing and enforcing professional standards of behavior removes some of the fuel which can turn small

disagreements into large fights. The standards should include guidelines to avoid:
- gossip,
- personal attacks,
- favoritism.

You can't eliminate conflict with this approach. It does not directly impact the causes of the conflict, but addresses the background environment. It discourages behavior that feeds conflict.

Emily asks Nat for more information about his unofficial code of conduct. See how he replies.

Nat: Well, there's nothing complicated. We just worked out the kinds of behavior that encouraged conflict, and then picked out the aspects that we could control.

It all focused on the way that people relate to their colleagues.

Emily: Such as?

Nat: We looked at the causes of the petty disputes, and found that a lot stemmed from rumors. For example, somebody said that I was up for a promotion, and the next thing, three people were annoyed that they didn't get it. And it wasn't true!

Emily: I see. So, no gossip or unfounded rumors.

Nat: No. And when I was supposedly about to be promoted, people made comments about how I "sneaked past" everyone else. So we avoid personal attacks now, and talk about professional competence only.

Emily: And that helps?

Nat: You'd be amazed. We still fight with each other, but the conflicts are so much more productive when it's not personal. Lastly, we introduced a "no favoritism" rule. We found that if you judge everyone and everything on merit alone, then when we do disagree, it's easier to handle.

Nat: No one gets annoyed, thinking that someone got treated better out of favoritism. People accept comments and criticism more willingly.

Question

Emily takes Nat's ideas back to her own organization, and tries to explain them to her colleagues at a team meeting. How should she describe the techniques for transforming an atmosphere that encourages conflict?

Options:

1. "We need to stop disagreeing with each other."
2. "It's important to stamp out favoritism."
3. "We must stop encouraging rumor and gossip."
4. "We all need to treat each other as friends."
5. "We have to avoid making personal comments."
6. "We have to ensure that we stand up for each other."

Answer:

In fact, preventing gossip, favoritism, and personal attacks are the main ways to transform an atmosphere of destructive conflict.

Option 1: This choice is incorrect because this is an unrealistic goal. Disagreements are an inevitable part of life.

Option 2: This is a correct choice. To create an atmosphere with less conflict, favoritism should be eliminated. When people are judged on merit alone, it's easier to handle disagreements.

Option 3: This option is correct. To make a work atmosphere more positive, rumors and gossip must be eliminated. Rumors and gossip can cause petty disputes, which can lead to more significant conflicts.

Option 4: This is incorrect. Treating each other as friends may actually lead to more conflict, not less. Friends may gossip and spread rumors about people outside their circle. It's best to keep work relationships professional.

Option 5: This choice is correct. Refraining from personal attacks minimizes conflict and creates a positive work environment.

Option 6: This option is not correct. Standing up for each other may actually fuel conflict, especially if people take sides against another person.

Nat and his colleagues drew up a detailed set of guidelines to ensure that destructive conflict didn't flourish in their company.

The guidelines also provided details of the kinds of behavior that they wanted to encourage. See each section of the document to reveal excerpts from these guidelines.

Avoid personal attacks

To avoid personal attacks on others, concentrate on performance issues, not character. Disagree with the idea, not the person, and use unemotional language. This is difficult when you are the one being attacked, but that's when it's most important.

Avoid gossip

Don't gossip. If you want to criticize someone, do it directly. Do not pass on unofficial rumors, and do not seek unofficial comments from colleagues. Stick to the known facts. Do not speculate.

Avoid favoritism

Treat everyone fairly and on the basis of merit. Do not make assumptions on the basis of past behavior, either good or bad. Favor no one. If you think that someone will disagree with you, explain why you are acting as you are.

The atmosphere of conflict in many organizations is pervasive and destructive. Now you know how to transform that atmosphere by changing how you behave with colleagues, and thereby setting a good example.

CHAPTER THREE
Managing Organization Conflict

Prevention of Conflict

Can you prevent conflict in the workplace? Well, maybe not entirely, but taking a preventative approach can be a sensible tactic for managers.

In fact, you may not want to eradicate all conflict because some conflict is healthy. It actually energizes. What you really want to do is prevent unhealthy, negative conflict. So what's the difference between organizations with healthy conflict and organizations with the type of conflict that should be prevented?

One of the most obvious ways of preventing conflict lies in attempting to eliminate the causes of conflict in the workplace. This simple recipe is based on the assumption that if you remove the causes of conflict, then it will not occur.

But despite its apparent simplicity, eradicating the causes of conflict is in fact a more complex process. As a manager, you need to be analytical and practical in deciding which causes of conflict you can and should attempt to remove.

Has anyone ever criticized you for your behavior but then acted in the same manner? If that has happened to you, you probably thought poorly of that person, and you probably didn't change your behavior at all. Well, that's similar to a real challenge you will face as a manager.

Not only do you have to tell your team members how you want them to behave, you have to live up to that behavior all the time. This is as true with managing conflict as it is with any other managerial task.

It takes two to fight. So it's apparent that if, as a manager, you can teach either or both of the disputants how to conduct themselves so they don't end up in destructive conflict, then it is time well spent.

Interpersonal skills training is a very effective way to prevent conflict in the workplace.

Benefits of preventing conflict in the workplace

Can you prevent conflict in the workplace? Well, maybe not entirely, but taking a preventative approach can be a sensible tactic for managers.

In fact, you may not want to eradicate all conflict because some conflict is healthy. It actually energizes. What you really want to do is prevent unhealthy, negative conflict. So what's the difference between organizations with healthy conflict and organizations with the type of conflict that should be prevented?

See each organization to find out more about each type of conflict.

Mercury Aggregates - Unhealthy conflict

In this organization, conflict is the norm and everything is mired in petty, uncontrolled disputes. This reduces production levels and requires managerial time.

Preston Holdings - Healthy conflict

Conflict does happen here, but only sporadically. Then it is either an indicator of something significant or a challenge to workplace complacency.

So you are aiming for a prevention of conflict to a level at which conflicts that do occur will be recognized as something exceptional.

You need to apply conflict-prevention techniques to situations like the one at Mercury Aggregates. You still won't eradicate all conflict, but you will gain considerable benefits from attempting to prevent it. You will

- recognize that if conflict does occur, it is signaling something important.
- feel assured that when conflict does occur, it is much more likely to be of the healthy variety.
- eliminate time-wasting managerial interventions to deal with constant conflict in your organization.

Question

Julie isn't sure about the benefits of trying to prevent conflict. What should you say to her about those benefits?

Options:

1. "Conflict takes a lot of time to deal with. So although trying to prevent it takes time, you will still save time by not wasting it on unnecessary squabbles."

2. "The benefit is obvious. You won't have any conflict left to deal with."

3. "You can recognize that when conflict happens, it's pointing out something important."

4. "You'll be able to feel confident that conflict in your organization is usually the healthy kind."

Answer:

In fact, by preventing conflict, you can remove the negative forms of conflict to leave the positive forms, which indicate something you really need to be concerned about. And you'll spend less time on unnecessary squabbles.

Option 1: This option is correct. One of the benefits of implementing conflict-prevention techniques is eliminating the need for time-consuming managerial interventions to deal with constant strife in your organization.

Option 2: This option is incorrect. Applying conflict-prevention techniques, no matter how effective, will not eliminate conflict altogether. It is virtually impossible to wipe out conflict in organizations.

Option 3: This choice is correct. When you apply conflict-prevention strategies in your organization, you'll know that if conflict does occur, it indicates something important.

Option 4: This is correct. When you apply conflict-prevention techniques, you'll feel confident that when conflict does arise, it is much more likely to be of the healthy variety.

So you don't need to worry if you have conflict in your organization. What you need to do is distinguish between positive and negative conflict and try to prevent the latter.

Eradicating the causes of conflict

One of the most obvious ways of preventing conflict lies in attempting to eliminate the causes of conflict in the workplace. This simple recipe is based on the assumption that if you remove the causes of conflict, then it will not occur.

But despite its apparent simplicity, eradicating the causes of conflict is in fact a more complex process. As a manager, you need to be analytical and practical in deciding which causes of conflict you can and should attempt to remove. Here are three categories of causes of conflict:

- causes that result in beneficial conflict,
- causes that you cannot control as a manager,
- causes that you can control and do want to eradicate because they lead to negative conflict.

The first two categories you either should not or cannot eliminate. You should not try to eliminate the causes of conflict that have a positive value. This sort of conflict, caused by high professional standards, for example, challenges complacency and careless working practices.

Some causes of conflict you cannot eliminate because they are outside your sphere of influence. For example, you cannot remove conflict caused by pay comparisons among workers if you do not set the company pay rates.

Instead you need to concentrate on the third category: causes you control and want to eradicate. In this category, the major factor is role conflict. Role conflict occurs when duties performed by a worker clash with those of other workers. As a manager, you can expect to exercise a considerable amount of control over the roles your employees play, so you can have great influence in eradicating this cause of conflict.

See each aspect to learn more information about role conflict.

Role ambiguity

Role ambiguity occurs when workers are uncertain of their actual duties. A task may not be completed because no one knows who is responsible for it, or workers may argue with each other over who is responsible.

Role demands

When workers have either too many or too few expectations placed on them, they may end up in conflict situations because they cannot complete the tasks assigned to them or because they feel unchallenged.

Role incompatibility

Role incompatibility occurs when contradictory expectations are placed on workers. They are expected to perform certain tasks, but at the same time conflicting demands are placed upon them. This usually results in poor performance.

Mary, Cole, and Ryan have experienced role conflict in the workplace. They have been interviewed by a consultant trying to advise managers on ways to eradicate the causes of conflict in the workplace. Select the employees' names to learn what they have to say.

Mary

"I'm so angry. I've just completed the quarter returns, which takes forever, and Ernesto tells me that he's been working on it for the last two weeks. I asked my boss whose job it was, and he just looked confused. It turned out that neither of us were officially supposed to do it."

Cole

"I'm just overwhelmed by my job. There's so much to do that I don't know what to do first. Last week I was told to sort out the expenses, but then half the staff members were angry because I hadn't been working on their bonus payments--so they were late."

Ryan

"Do you know Charlie just yelled at me because he said I was supposed to be helping him with the filing? Then Norman told Charlie that he was wrong, and I should be working with him to do the audit. The next thing I know they're having a huge argument in front of everybody."

Jenny, the consultant who interviewed Mary, Cole, and Ryan, not only has to explain to their managers the way that problems with staff roles can cause conflict but also what they should do to deal with it.

See each role type for an explanation of Jenny's recommendations.

Role ambiguity

"To remedy role ambiguity, you need to precisely define all roles and make sure that individual responsibilities are clearly communicated. Roles develop spontaneously, so you need to update this information on a regular basis."

Role demands

"If your employees feel that the expectations of them are unfair, you need to examine each one's quantity of work and distribute it evenly. You must explain the way that tasks have been prioritized and insist that workers stick to this pattern."

Role incompatibility

"When A thinks that B is going to do something but B doesn't know that, you've got problems. So get A and B talking about what they expect of each other. Then you'll know what the hidden problems are, and you'll be able to sort them out."

Case Study: Question 1 of 3
Scenario:
You are the manager of a small office.

The staff members are growing increasingly argumentative with each other, and more and more disputes are coming to your attention.

You resolve to try to eradicate some of these problems by reducing role conflict among team members. Answer the following questions to show how you will do this.

Question:
Colin and Maggie aren't speaking to each other. Maggie agreed that one of her team members could attend a conference on e-learning without telling Colin. Colin, who has been in charge of staff training, was annoyed when Maggie approved the visit. How will you eradicate this conflict?

Options:
1. The problem is that both of them think employee training is their responsibility. I would define their roles in relation to training more clearly.

2. I'd eradicate this conflict by stopping all employee training for Maggie's team for the immediate future. 3. I'd make sure that Colin and Maggie recognize that both of them need to understand each other's responsibility in organizing training.

4. I'd tell Ellis to take over training and assume that he'd tell Colin and Maggie.

Answer:
In fact, role definition and ascertaining responsibilities attached to roles are the ways to eradicate conflict.

Option 1: This is correct. The solution addresses the conflict between Colin and Maggie by remedying role ambiguity. When they clearly understand their roles with relation to staff training, the cause of the conflict will be removed.

Option 2: This choice is incorrect. Although this may temporarily solve the problem, it is not a long-term solution. The conflict will arise when Maggie's team resumes employee training.

Option 3: This option is correct. If Colin and Maggie understand each other's responsibilities in organizing training, their conflict should be eradicated. When individual responsibilities are clearly communicated, role conflict disappears.

Option 4: This option is incorrect because changing the person who is in charge of training will not address role ambiguity. Without clearly defined roles, Ellis and Maggie are likely to run into the same problems as those between Colin and Maggie.

Case Study: Question 2 of 3

Prakash wants to talk to you because he has been arguing with his colleagues about workload. They feel that he has been given less responsibility than the other team members but is receiving the same wages, and they are angry with him about it. What should you do to eradicate the cause of this conflict?

Options:

1. I must give Prakash more work to stop the others from complaining.

2. I need to look at the demands of all of their roles to compare workloads.

3. I must ensure that the workloads of staff members are comparatively equal.

4. I must take some work off the other staff members so that they won't think that Prakash has a better deal.

Answer:

Actually, to avoid creating conflict, role demands need to be analyzed to ensure equality.

Option 1: This option is incorrect because you must first examine the workloads of Prakash and his colleagues before reassigning work.

Option 2: This choice is correct. Because Prakash's colleagues feel that the workload isn't evenly distributed, you should compare role demands to establish equity and to avoid conflict.

Option 3: This option is correct. After assessing current role demands, you should distribute the work evenly among Prakash and his colleagues.

Option 4: This choice is incorrect because you must first assess the role demands of Prakash and his colleagues before reducing workloads. You should establish equity in role demand if the conflict is to be avoided.

Case Study: Question 3 of 3

Connie tells you that Eric has been very rude to her because she has not completed the staff absentee report since Estelle went on vacation. Connie explains that she didn't know she was supposed to cover for Estelle. What should you do to eradicate the cause of this conflict?

Options:

1. I would make sure that all unspoken expectations about roles were discussed so that employees know what other employees think they should be doing.

2. I would identify any problems that might arise because of expectations of other employees and eliminate them.

3. I would tell Connie that she had better take over the staff absentee report from now on.

4. I would tell Eric that he shouldn't be rude to other members of the staff and ask him to apologize.

Answer:

In fact, if you eliminate any role incompatibility by getting people to discuss their expectations and then removing the potential clashes, you will remove this cause of conflict.

Option 1: This option is correct. It is best to ask employees to discuss their expectations about roles so as to eliminate role ambiguity.

Option 2: This choice is correct. After employees have discussed their expectations, you should deal with any clashes pertaining to role expectations. This will eliminate any conflicts that may have arisen.

Option 3: This is incorrect. Although this solution would address the problem in Estelle's absence, it would create role ambiguity when she returned.

Option 4: Incorrect. Directing Eric to curb his rudeness will not address the underlying problem--role ambiguity and unspoken expectations. He may stop his rude behavior, but he'll still be upset because he believes that Connie is shirking her duties.

By tackling role conflict head on, you can eliminate one of the major causes of conflict that lies in your direct sphere of influence as a manager.

A collaborative approach

Has anyone ever criticized you for your behavior but then acted in the same manner? If that has happened to you, you probably thought poorly of that person, and you probably didn't change your behavior at all. Well, that's similar to a real challenge you will face as a manager.

Not only do you have to tell your team members how you want them to behave, you have to live up to that behavior all the time. This is as true with managing conflict as it is with any other managerial task.

Your behavior must signal to your team an approach to conflict that encourages the positive aspects of it and discourages the negative parts. This means developing and maintaining a collaborative culture. A collaborative culture is based on:

- honest communication,
- respect shown to everyone,
- a positive attitude toward constructive conflict.

Tania thinks that Errol, her manager, maintains a collaborative culture with his behavior. Here's why.

Tania: You know how you stand with Errol because he tells you. There are no hidden secrets. Errol really respects his team, and that's what he expects from everyone. But the thing I like most about him is that he's not afraid of being challenged. If you've got a good point to make, you can argue with Errol. He encourages it.

So how would Errol describe his approach to his team?

Errol developed his approach based on his experiences working for many different managers. He admired some of them, but others showed him what he shouldn't do.

See each characteristic for an example of Errol's approach.

Respect

"Respect is vital--show it and you'll get it. And respect has to be universal. I've worked in too many places where respect is reserved for those higher up than you. That's not right. You need to show respect to everyone in the organization."

Positive attitude toward constructive conflict

"I've worked in places where you can't disagree. If you're scared to debate, your team members can't learn how to have a positive attitude about conflict. I encourage them to disagree with me, and I show them how you can learn from it."

Honest communication

"In many workplaces, there are too many secrets and assumptions. If I'm going to do something that affects my team members, I tell them, even if they don't like it. And I ask them what they think. I've learned my lesson. I don't make assumptions."

But the real proof that Errol has created a collaborative culture has to come from the testimonies of his team members, who have experienced on a day-to-day basis the approach that Errol uses with them and their colleagues.

We've seen what Tania thinks.

See the names of Tania's colleagues to find out what they think about Errol's approach to his team.

Vikram

"Errol definitely does what he asks us to do. He's big on respect. My best example of this is the way he behaves toward the janitors. He invites them to the team meetings and social events. He says that they're part of the team and should have their say."

Fallon

"I'm new, so I've been quiet. I was there when Tania was talking about software licenses. Her proposal sounded illegal, but that's her area of expertise. I wasn't going to say anything until Errol said to me that because I'd put licensing experience on my resume, he wanted to know what I thought."

Alex

"Everybody thought I'd leave when I didn't get a promotion. So I went through this phase of being cut out of the loop unless I made a fuss. But Errol came straight out and said that I should tell him what my intentions were. He didn't want to make any assumptions. And he hasn't."

Question

Two managers, Cyril and Harry, are trying to pin down the characteristics of a collaborative approach to managing conflict in the workplace.

Which of the following statements describe this way of working?

Options:

1. You need to show respect for all workers in the organization.

2. You should avoid disagreeing with your team members.

3. Do not argue with other managers in public.

4. You must encourage constructive conflict.

5. Keep people well informed, and avoid making assumptions.

Answer:

Actually, to develop a culture of collaboration, you will need to communicate openly and show respect to all staff members. You must also encourage healthy debate as part of a collaborative approach.

Option 1: This choice is correct. To foster a collaborative culture, you must demonstrate respect toward everyone in the organization. To get respect, you must give it.

Option 2: This choice is not correct. Avoiding disagreements is not only impossible, but also not necessarily productive. When handled properly, disagreements can help build a collaborative culture.

Option 3: This option is incorrect because there is no advantage for managers to argue in private. Managers should model constructive conflict so employees can learn to have a positive attitude about conflict.

Option 4: This is correct. Modeling and encouraging a positive attitude about conflict will help establish a collaborative culture.

Option 5: This choice is correct. Secrets and assumptions can undermine a culture of collaboration. It is best to communicate openly and honestly and to question assumptions.

If you ask Errol how he collaborates with his team, he finds the question a little odd; for him it's obvious. "You just treat people properly," he replies.

But if he's pushed a little, he can describe what he does and point out the best ways to develop a collaborative approach.

See each characteristic for examples of Errol's collaborative approach.

Respect

"If you respect someone, you treat that person as an equal. It's more than politeness; that can just be patronizing. You need to ask people what they think because you value different perspectives. You don't have to agree with them."

Positive attitude toward constructive conflict

"When we talk about how we do things and someone starts to criticize a certain practice, I stop them. I insist that you can criticize a colleague only if you have a better solution to offer. That really makes our arguments positive and productive."

Honest communication

"I'm totally open with my team members. That doesn't mean I tell them everything, but I am always honest. And I'm quite happy if they push me. I'll push them. I don't wait to be told; I ask. I'm an active communicator."

Creating a collaborative culture through your own actions is essential if you wish to encourage the positive aspects of argument and disagreement in your organization.

Interpersonal skills training

It takes two to fight. So it's apparent that if, as a manager, you can teach either or both of the disputants how to conduct themselves so they don't end up in destructive conflict, then it is time well spent.

Interpersonal skills training is a very effective way to prevent conflict in the workplace.

There are many aspects of interpersonal skills training. The ones that are most relevant to the prevention of conflict are:
- enabling your team members to understand their instinctive approaches to conflict,
- developing communication skills,
- showing how to collaborate.

This approach to training is based on getting your team members to assess the way they respond to conflict and helping them to behave differently if necessary. It is not saying that they must follow a fixed formula that will apply in all situations.

Select each company for an example of effective interpersonal skills training programs that prevent conflict.

B A Loans

Staff members at BA Loans recover delinquent debts and often face conflict with clients. As part of their training, they're given a test that analyzes their attitude toward conflict, and then they're debriefed by a psychologist.

Hammond and Harwood

Communication skills are the center of training at Hammond & Harwood. Managers believe that poor communication causes a lot of conflict, so they want employees to listen, question, and show understanding of one another's views.

Exeedo

Collaboration is the goal at Exeedo, but the training manager believes that won't happen unless employees are shown how to work with each other to mutually solve problems. He gives them training in integrative bargaining techniques.

Question

Warren believes that interpersonal skills training needs to be based on effective communication skills; Tyler thinks an attitude test examining your response to conflict is essential; Bobbie Sue says the training should provide a five-point plan for preventing conflict in all situations; and Dion says that to prevent conflict, you need to know how to collaborate. Which of them are describing important elements of interpersonal skills training to prevent conflict?

Options:
1. Warren
2. Tyler
3. Bobbie Sue
4. Dion

Answer:

Actually, the essential components of interpersonal skills training to prevent conflict are effective communication, attitude surveys, and collaborative techniques.

Option 1: This is correct. Warren describes one element of interpersonal skills training that prevents conflict. Communication must be two-way to prevent conflict.

Option 2: This option is correct. Tyler describes an important element in interpersonal skills training. Attitude testing provides information about how people will react to conflict based on their test results.

Option 3: This option is not correct. What Bobbie Sue describes is not part of interpersonal skills training for conflict prevention. There is no plan that prevents conflict in all situations. Preventing conflict in all situations is virtually impossible.

Option 4: This is correct. Dion describes collaboration, an element in interpersonal skills training for conflict prevention. This is an approach that prioritizes achieving an acceptable outcome for all.

Some people argue that people cannot really change the way they behave. Others believe that interpersonal skills are skills that can be taught in a way similar to the way someone can be taught to play the piano. This is the approach that is taken in this topic. If you take this approach to interpersonal skills training, then you do have to provide a detailed rationale for each element in the training to explain why it's vital.

See each training element to learn more.

Attitude tests

Attitude testing gives people feedback on the way they will react to conflict. This empowers the individual. If a person wants to change his behavior, he can. Part of this approach is the idea that behavioral change can only come from inside. People only change because they want to.

Communication skills

Communication must enable you to understand the other person's point of view and effectively present your own viewpoint. If either of these two elements fail, then the collaborative approach is jeopardized. Communication needs to be two-way to be effective in preventing conflict.

Collaborative techniques

Collaboration is a technique of balance that requires individuals to be assertive on their own behalf and concerned with achieving an acceptable outcome for all. These principles are more important than specific ways of acting because they can be adapted to fit a range of conflict situations.

Doug, Pritti, and Hester have taken interpersonal skills training to prevent conflict. Here they describe those experiences.

Doug: It was a revelation for me. I'd never really come to grips with conflict. I'd had some training, and I understood the techniques, but I couldn't use them back at work. Then I had to complete a questionnaire that got me thinking about the way I really react to other people when I'm arguing with them.

Pritti: So what difference did that make?

Doug: Well, with help I could find out how passive I was and how much I

wanted to change. Until then I'd just been going through the motions.

Pritti: I feel the same way, but my breakthrough was more simple. I had a session on collaborations, and for once it wasn't all about "do this--do that." It was more about principles, and when I got this win-win philosophy in my head, I was fine. I could work out the balance between assertion and keeping the relationship.

Hester: My experiences are similar. Only for me, the best part was looking at communication skills. I'd always thought I was a good listener, but nobody else thought so. So I really worked hard at improving my listening skills, and it works. If the communication is genuinely two-way, most conflict disappears.

Question

Donald must convince his CEO to spend money on interpersonal skills training to prevent conflict in the workplace. He is preparing an outline of the key elements in the training and bullet points about the rationale for each element. Match the key elements with the rationale.

Options:

A. attitude tests
B. communication skills
C. collaborative techniques

Targets:

1. a two-way process
2. based on principles of balance

3. empowers individuals
Answer:
Actually, the answers shown show how the elements of interpersonal skills training match with the rationales for them.

Communication skills for conflict prevention require a two-way process. Each person must be able to effectively convey his point of view and understand the other's perspective.

Collaboration techniques are based on principles of balance that require individuals to simultaneously advance their own interests and be concerned with achieving an acceptable outcome for all involved parties.

Attitude testing empowers individuals by providing feedback on the way they will respond to conflict. This feedback can be used by individuals to change their behavior and to improve the way they deal with conflict.

Do you want to help your team manage conflict more effectively? Then the pattern of interpersonal skills training suggested here is just what you need to do it.

Conflict Reduction and Containment

In an ideal world, managers would always attempt to resolve any difficulties they encounter with long- term and permanent solutions. Unfortunately, we do not live in an ideal world, so managers sometimes need to go for "quick fixes."

Quick fixes are solutions that treat the symptoms but are not concerned with finding a cure. In terms of managing conflict, quick fixes are reduction and containment techniques.

What is management? Of course, it's many things and has many definitions. Henri Fayol said that to manage is to forecast and plan, to organize, to command, to coordinate, and to control. So one aspect of management is exercising control through commanding your team.

In other words, if members of the staff are involved in an action and you want to stop them, one of the simplest ways is to ask them to stop. If they do, that's fine, but occasionally they will not. Then you will have to insist.

Arbitration is hearing both sides of an argument and then deciding between them. It is a useful way to manage disputes in the organization because by exercising authority in this way, the manager contains the conflict.

A couple of colleagues who can't agree may ask co-workers to help them resolve the conflict. But it's different when a manager acts as an arbiter--managers are more like referees.

Mediation and arbitration are often confused, but the biggest difference between the two lies in the intervention style of the manager.

Arbitration is an enforced decision made by the manager to resolve the disagreement. During mediation, a manager negotiates an agreement that both parties in the dispute are willing to agree to. Effective mediation requires three distinct elements.

Reducing and containing conflicts

In an ideal world, managers would always attempt to resolve any difficulties they encounter with long- term and permanent solutions. Unfortunately, we do not live in an ideal world, so managers sometimes need to go for "quick fixes."

Managing Workplace Conflicts

Quick fixes are solutions that treat the symptoms but are not concerned with finding a cure. In terms of managing conflict, quick fixes are reduction and containment techniques.

Reduction and containment techniques are most useful in conflict situations that demand an immediate response.

Examples of these situations include:
- The conflict will interrupt essential production.
- You fear that the conflict will escalate and involve other team members.
- Your reputation requires you to show that you are addressing the problem.

These techniques won't work every time. Containment of a problem can mean that the pressure just builds up, so the eventual explosion is even bigger. But there are good reasons for managers to take these approaches:
- They will provide an immediate solution.
- They can be quickly implemented and repeated if necessary.
- They can be used for the less important issues so that more time can be spent on more significant problems.

Marvin has used reduction and containment techniques in his management of conflict. He knows the advantages and disadvantages. Here's what he has to say.

Sometimes I don't have room for the perfect solution. Dick and Sheree are always arguing, but they nearly came to blows last week. You stop that sort of thing right away.

No one on my team is going to question my authority. I didn't just ask them to stop fighting--I made them stop.

Question

How should Marvin justify the quick-fix approach he sometimes takes to managing conflict to his boss, Celia?

Options:

1. "I can sideline less important problems this way."
2. "It demarcates the problem."
3. "It allows the pressure to build."
4. "It provides an immediate solution."
5. "I can repeat my actions if I need to."

Answer:

In fact, the benefits of applying reduction and containment techniques lie in speed, repetition, and prioritization.

Option 1: This choice is correct. One of the benefits of applying reduction and containment techniques is that less significant problems can be tabled, so more significant issues can be addressed.

Option 2: This is incorrect. Marvin should not mention this as a benefit of reduction and containment techniques. Demarcating the problem requires problem-definition strategies and is outside the scope of reduction and containment techniques.

Option 3: This is incorrect. Marvin should not mention this to Celia because this is actually a downside of containment. Containment of a problem can result in pressure building up, so the eventual explosion is even greater.

Option 4: This is correct. Marvin should highlight the fact that reduction and containment techniques are the most useful in conflict situations that demand an immediate response. Sometimes, managers must go for quick fixes.

Option 5: This choice is correct. Marvin should mention the benefit of being able to quickly implement and repeat reduction and containment techniques, if necessary.

Managers have to deal with conflict, and they need a variety of techniques to do so. These techniques work really well in some situations, so you need them in your armory to be effective at managing conflict in the workplace.

Coercion

What is management? Of course, it's many things and has many definitions. Henri Fayol said that to manage is to forecast and plan, to organize, to command, to coordinate, and to control. So one aspect of management is exercising control through commanding your team.

In other words, if members of the staff are involved in an action and you want to stop them, one of the simplest ways is to ask them to stop. If they do, that's fine, but occasionally they will not. Then you will have to insist.

This is the beginning of coercion. Coercion means making somebody do something by force, and the force that managers apply is in the form of official organizational sanctions.

Coercion is a technique for managing conflict that is most likely to be used as an interim stage on the way to finding a longer-term and more profound solution. It does not attempt anything more than containment of the problem.

Usually it will be of most use in extreme situations.

See each situation to learn more about when coercion should be used.

Passions

One of the most obvious uses of coercive techniques is when people have become irrational. The argument has become so passionate that they cannot be stopped by anything other than an extreme response, such as some form of sanction.

False compliance

A manager may need to use coercion when the people in conflict have repeatedly pretended to stop when asked to do so, but in fact have continued the behavior. The argument has become more important than the manager's authority.

Testing out

Use coercion when the conflict is immaterial to all parties, but it is being used as an excuse to covertly challenge your will and authority. Then the full range of the technique may need to be applied to show control.

Janet, Trevor, and George have used coercion to manage conflict in their teams. Here are their stories.

Janet: I'd really never come across anything like it before. I heard the noise from down the corridor, and by the time I got into their office, Frank and Dave had completely lost their tempers. They were screaming at each other, and I couldn't get them to stop. Finally I threatened them with suspension, and that stopped them.

Trevor: The fifth time that the staff meeting was interrupted because of an argument between Jess and Gloria, I finally stopped it. They had promised before not to keep arguing, but each time they did. This time I told them I'd remove them from the meeting if they did it again.

Managing Workplace Conflicts

George: Jerry and Karl have been with the company for years, long before I started. I knew that because I was so much younger than they were that they didn't have much respect for my authority. So when the quarrels between them were manufactured just to test me, I made sure they knew who was in charge.

Question

Henry doesn't really understand when he is most likely to need coercion as a way to manage conflict in his organization. Which of the following situations would describe the circumstances for being coercive?

Options:

1. people are only pretending to comply with his requests
2. people refuse to talk about a compromise
3. people are using conflict to test his managerial authority
4. people have become irrational
5. people argue with him

Answer:

Actually, coercion is best used when passions are very high. Henry may also have to use it when he has been ignored or is being tested.

Option 1: This is correct. Henry should use coercion when the people in conflict repeatedly pretend to stop when asked to do so, but continue the behavior.

Option 2: This is incorrect. Coercion is not the appropriate reaction when Henry encounters people who refuse to compromise. Henry may need to intervene when people refuse to talk about a compromise, but not in such an extreme way.

Option 3: This is correct. Henry should use coercion when the conflict is immaterial to all parties but being used as an excuse to covertly challenge his will and authority. Then, the full range of the technique may need to be applied to show control.

Option 4: This is correct. Coercion should be used to put an end to an argument that has become irrational and out of control. An extreme response is required in this situation.

Option 5: This choice is not correct. There is no need for Henry to use coercion when people argue with him. Coercion would be an inappropriate reaction, unless the argument was becoming explosive.

The coercive response to resolving conflict is not only best applied in certain situations, but it also has to be cautiously applied as an extreme measure. This means that you should not rush to a full-blown coercive response; you should lead up to it with a graduated response that moves through three stages of severity, depending on the reaction of the protagonists in the conflict.

If a request to stop the conflict has been ignored, then as a manager, you must insist with increasing force. As the protagonists continue to ignore your attempts to resolve the problem, your responses must progress accordingly.

See each stage of resolution attempt to learn more.

Tell

Telling isn't that different from asking, except in the way you phrase and emphasize your statement. This doesn't mean being impolite, but you are now insisting, not asking. Very often this change in tone will be sufficient to bring people to their senses.

Threaten

Unfortunately, passions tend to rule conflict, so you may need to spell out the consequences of ignoring your instructions. This needs to be an appropriate response that is within your authority. You must remain calm and in control.

Apply sanctions

You must be able and willing to impose any sanction you threaten. The rarity of this situation shouldn't diminish your resolve to act as you've said you will. By ignoring you, your team members have forced your hand, and when necessary, you must show them you are in control.

Applying sanctions is a last resort, but on rare occasions you will have to use them. Managing conflict has now become mixed up with your general authority as a manager. So how will you stop conflict between very difficult employees?

Case Study: Question 1 of 3
Scenario:

For your convenience, the case study is repeated with each question.

Damian has been transferred to your team and is under your direct supervision. He has a reputation for being very committed to his work. You overhear Damian having a loud argument with Eve about the report she has written. Damian is tearing up the report as you walk in. You ask them both to calm down and tell you what is going on. Damian takes no notice of you and continues to shout at Eve.

How should you deal with this conflict? Answer the following questions in order.

Question:

Damian has really lost his temper and sweeps all the papers off his desk onto the floor.

What should you say to Damian to stop him from continuing this argument?

Options:

1. I should shout even louder than Damian in an attempt to shut him up.

2. I should tell Damian to stop it immediately and sit down.

3. I should continue to ask Damian to please stop shouting.

Answer:

You must tell Damian to stop in a firm and controlled way.

Option 1: This option is incorrect. You are being impolite by shouting at Damian before insisting that he stop his argument.

Option 2: This is correct because this is a firm statement, emphasizing what you want Damian to do. Now, Damian has a clear direction to follow.

Option 3: This choice is not correct. This response requires a more emphatic and direct tone for Damian to take it seriously. If you use this approach, Damian will probably continue his behavior.

Case Study: Question 2 of 3

Your response has no effect on Damian, and he continues to shout at Eve.

As his manager, what should you now do to stop the argument?

Options:

1. I should grab his arm and pull him out of the room until he stops shouting.

2. I should tell him that I will never let anyone else work with him again if he doesn't stop.

3. I should tell him that this is harassment and that I will suspend him immediately if he does not stop.

Answer:

Actually, the way to stop Damian is to threaten an appropriate sanction.

Option 1: This choice is incorrect because using physical force to remove Damian from the room is an inappropriate response that demonstrates your loss of resolve.

Option 2: This option is not correct. Although this threat may have some shock value, it is highly unlikely that you will be able to implement such a sanction in these circumstances.

Option 3: This choice is correct because it clearly and calmly tells Damian what sanctions you will implement if he does not stop shouting.

Case Study: Question 3 of 3

Damian doesn't pay any attention to you. He is still shouting at Eve.

What should you do now?

Options:

1. I should call the security guards to enforce an immediate suspension from work.

2. I should tell Eve to sit down, ignore him, and carry on with the report as though nothing has happened.

3. I should repeat my threat to never let anyone else work with him again if he doesn't stop.

Answer:

Actually, if you have threatened a sanction and Damian still does not stop, then you must apply that sanction.

Option 1: This choice is correct because you have applied the sanction--suspending Damian from work--and stopped the conflict. You gave Damian plenty of chances to stop the conflict before applying this sanction.

Option 2: This option is not correct. This strategy does not deal with the fact that Damian is out of control. If Eve ignores him, it may escalate the conflict.

Option 3: This is incorrect because this same threat would not have stopped Damian's behavior earlier. Further, you may not be able to carry out this threat. This course of action may diminish your authority.

Coercion isn't going to cure conflict, and it's not intended to. But in some situations, managers have to stop conflict before they can try to cure it. This is where coercion comes in.

If you have to deal with staff members who do not stop their behavior when you ask them to, now you know how to effectively coerce them into stopping.

Arbitration

Arbitration is hearing both sides of an argument and then deciding between them. It is a useful way to manage disputes in the organization because by exercising authority in this way, the manager contains the conflict.

A couple of colleagues who can't agree may ask co-workers to help them resolve the conflict. But it's different when a manager acts as an arbiter--managers are more like referees. When managers arbitrate:
- they do not have to be invited; they have official power and authority to intervene.
- they do not have to reach a solution that either or both of the parties agree to.

- their decision is binding.

When Oliver and Curtis couldn't agree on the recommendations for a report, their manager, Ruth, intervened.

Oliver: We were meeting with her to discuss the recommendations, and Curtis and I saw things very differently. I wasn't too sure how we would bridge the gap. But then Ruth said she had heard our arguments, and now she was going to decide on the recommendations.

Curtis: I was pretty shocked. I told her that we hadn't asked her to do that, but she said that wasn't the issue. The report had to be completed and we couldn't agree, so she was sorting it out. And she did. End of argument.

Arbitration is acting as an authority figure. But arbitration conversely is most successful when the disputing parties are happy with, and accepting of, the decision you impose. That way, not only is your decision more likely to be carried out by them, but it also will have a more positive influence on your future arbitrations. So you need to make sure that the arbitration has certain characteristics.

See each characteristic of arbitration to learn more about them.

Working with both sides

This does not mean that the disputants necessarily actively participate in the decision you reach, but they should feel that they have been engaged with the process. This must apply equally to both sides, and each party must feel that he had a chance to voice his concerns.

Making justifiable decisions

The decision you reach must be based on justifiable facts and reasons, not on arbitrary opinions and feelings.

Then even people who disagree with you will be able to understand the legitimacy of your reasoning.

Getting buy-in from both sides

If you can get buy-in from both parties, this will be beneficial to arbitration now and in the future. You may have to spend extra time on the process, ensuring that your reasoning is public knowledge and offering explanations as to why you discounted other solutions.

Enabling a win-win situation

If the disputants feel positive about the process and the way you have engaged them, they will be advocates of arbitration. Their acceptance can encourage a positive attitude about it throughout the organization.

Question

Harvey knows that as a manager acting as an arbiter, he needs to understand four important characteristics of successful arbitration.

Match each characteristic of successful arbitration with its related description.

Options:

A. working with both sides
B. making justifiable decisions
C. getting buy-in from both sides
D. enabling a win-win situation

Targets:

1. protagonists are the best advocates
2. doesn't mean they participate in the decision-making
3. based on reasoned arguments
4. takes additional time

Answer:

Actually, the correct answers match the four characteristics of successful arbitration with the phrases that describe them.

By enabling a win-win situation, protagonists become the best advocates. If the disputants feel positive about the process, they will be advocates of arbitration within your organization.

Working with both sides does not mean that the disputants actively participate in the final decision, but they should feel that they have been involved in the process. Each party must feel that he had a chance to express his concerns.

Justifiable decisions are based on reasoned arguments, not on arbitrary opinions and feelings. That way, even those who disagree with you will be able to understand the legitimacy of your reasoning.

Getting buy-in from both sides may take additional time. But if you can get buy-in from both parties, it will be beneficial to arbitration now and in the future.

Whatever style of arbitration a manager follows, part of the goal is to contain the conflict as successfully as possible. Containing the conflict successfully depends in part on the way the manager acts when conducting the arbitration.

You need to consider four techniques for acting as an arbiter that will help to prolong the containment of the conflict.

See each technique for acting as an arbiter to learn more.

Listening

Whatever decision you come to, you must ensure that all parties feel they have been given a fair hearing. This means listening to their complete arguments without any form of prejudgments and avoiding at all costs any form of favoritism.

Making rational decisions

You'll contain the conflict longer if your decision is rational and can be justified by facts. But the competitive nature of conflict means that opposing parties may accept a decision more easily if it has emotional appeal, such as being good for the company.

Persuading

Although arbitration is based upon your authority, you should persuade the parties involved of the rightness of the decision. If you can persuade them to see the decision as effective, you won't need to coerce them to accept it, and you'll get a long-term solution.

Saving face

Another arbitration technique is to allow each side to save face. You can do this by adopting any element of their approach that fits with your decision and asking them to be involved in the implementation of the decision.

Case Study: Question 1 of 2

Scenario:

For your convenience, the case study is repeated with each question.

Garth and his team share the office with Sylvia and her team. They have been fighting about the lack of space for months. You are their manager, and with an important visitor coming, you want to sort out the problems and end the fighting.

You call Garth and Sylvia into your office to arbitrate in the quarrel between them. Answer the following questions, in order, using arbitration techniques correctly.

Managing Workplace Conflicts

Question:

Sylvia immediately complains that you have always favored Garth because he's a friend of your daughter, and so she knows whom you will favor. She says there's no way she can agree to support a decision made on those terms. How should you reply to Sylvia?

Options:

1. Sylvia, before you attack me even more, let me tell you that it doesn't do your case any good.

2. I haven't heard either of your arguments yet. The first thing I want to do is listen to both of you.

3. I can't win in that case, because if I side with Garth, you will just dismiss it as favoritism. So I'll just try to sort out what seems right.

4. Sylvia, the decision I make will be based on the facts and will have nothing to do with friendships.

Answer:

In fact, to make the arbitration more effective in containing conflict, it is essential to listen to both sides and to show that your argument is rationally founded.

Option 1: This option is incorrect. The fact that Sylvia is attacking you should be irrelevant. Your decision should be based on the facts of the case, not on Sylvia's behavior.

Option 2: This choice is correct. You need to listen to both sides so that Sylvia and Garth both feel as though they have had a fair hearing. And by listening to Sylvia's point of view, you'll show you are not favoring Garth.

Option 3: This option is incorrect. Just sorting out what seems right before listening to both arguments is not an effective approach. If you don't have the facts on which to base your decision, you will probably be influenced by favoritism.

Option 4: This choice is correct. By articulating your commitment to making a rational decision based on the full facts of the case, you are showing that you're not favoring Garth. Such a decision is likely to be accepted by both Garth and Sylvia.

Case Study: Question 2 of 2

Garth isn't happy with your decision to put him and his team into temporary accommodations until something more permanent can be found for them. He says that by trying to show Sylvia that you have been fair, you have ignored the case that he's made for Sylvia and her team moving out. How should you reply to him?

Options:

1. If the work is split so that your team only deals with the revenue accounts, then you can work independently from Sylvia. So you need to be located nearer the cash office.

2. I want you to choose the permanent office your team will move into.

3. Listen, it will all work to your advantage in the long run.

4. I'm going to split the work and give your team the easier jobs. That should compensate for your move.

Answer:

Actually, persuasion helps to make arbitration more palatable. Also, if you can involve the parties in the implementation, then they will feel ownership and be less likely to continue the argument.

Option 1: This option is correct. You are trying to persuade Garth of the merits of your decision by revealing your reasoning. Persuasion helps make arbitration more acceptable.

Option 2: This choice is correct. By involving Garth in the implementation process, you have increased the likelihood that this conflict will cease for a long time. He will feel more ownership and be less likely to continue the argument.

Option 3: This is incorrect. You have made no attempt to persuade Garth, so the conflict is much less likely to be contained.

Option 4: This is incorrect. This response neither persuades Garth of the rationale nor does it involve him in the implementation. Most likely, it will not give Garth a sense of ownership or fairness, so he may continue the conflict.

Arbitration is more than just making a decision. That's easy, but to persuade your team that it is the right decision and to get them to buy in requires the skills outlined here. Then arbitration will be effective in containing conflict.

Mediation

Mediation and arbitration are often confused, but the biggest difference between the two lies in the intervention style of the manager.

Arbitration is an enforced decision made by the manager to resolve the disagreement. During mediation, a manager negotiates an agreement that both parties in the dispute are willing to agree to. Effective mediation requires three distinct elements.

See each element to learn more about mediation.

Impartiality

It can be difficult for a manager to be seen as impartial. Usually, if the dispute is between two employees and one of them is in a higher position than the other, a manager would be expected to support the higher-ranking staff member.

Facilitation

Facilitation requires the manager to help his staff members to reach an agreement in the dispute by aiding the communication between them. This is a far less authoritative role than is required for arbitration.

Acceptance

Mediation requires managers to exercise less control of the outcome of the intervention. Managers may well find that they don't agree with the agreement the parties reach through mediation. But they must allow the parties to work it out.

Another part of the difference in style between arbitration and mediation is the time that the processes take. Because of the greater demands of a negotiated rather than an authoritative process, mediation is likely to require more of a manager's time. But even if this is the case, managers Clancy, Will, and Anne think it is time well spent.

See each manager to find out how they have successfully mediated in their organizations.

Clancy

"My co-manager, Erik, and Sherie, an administrator, had an argument over office procedures. It didn't seem likely that they would reach an agreement, so I stepped in and offered to mediate. I had to convince Sherie that I wouldn't naturally favor Erik, but we worked it out in the end."

Will

"The warehouse workers and the drivers refused to cooperate with each other, so I helped facilitate an agreement between them. I did it by utilizing a lot of behind-the-scenes talking. I knew if I tried to play 'boss', they would go back to their entrenched positions, so I just talked to them like one of the guys."

Anne

"I had to try hard not to say anything so many times when Artie and Sonia asked me to mediate, but it was worth it in the long run. The way they agreed to divide up the work seemed crazy to me. But it was what they thought would work best, and they were right. It has worked for them."

Question

James, Alex, Wilson, and Renee are office managers who are asked to describe some of the characteristics of mediation as a technique for managing conflict in their team.

Who is correct?

Options:

1. Alex says that the hardest part of mediation for her as a manager is losing control of the final agreement.

2. Wilson says that he prefers mediation because it is a lot quicker than arbitration.

3. Renee says that she finds it hard to take on the role of a mediator because she has to be far more facilitative and far less managerial.

4. James describes mediation as difficult because many staff members can't believe their manager can
be impartial.

Answer:

Actually, the characteristics are impartiality, facilitative skills, and a less controlling approach applied by the manager.

Option 1: Alex's comment correctly describes the mediation process. In mediation, managers have less control over the outcome. They may find that they disagree with the mediated agreement, but they must allow the parties to work it out.

Option 2: Wilson's comment is incorrect. Mediation is more time-consuming than arbitration because of the greater demands of a negotiated, as opposed to an authoritative, process.

Option 3: Renee's assertion is correct. Facilitation requires the manager to help her staff members reach an agreement in the dispute by helping them communicate. This is a far less authoritative role than is required for arbitration.

Option 4: James is correct. It may be difficult for a manager to be seen as impartial. For instance, if the dispute is between two employees at different levels in an organization, a manager would be expected to back the higher-ranking employee.

Clancy, Will, and Anne know that mediation is an effective but demanding process for a manager. They've developed such a reputation for being effective mediators that they've been asked to contribute an article called "The Gurus of Mediation" for the management web site. Each of them takes an aspect of the process and describes how a manager can be an effective mediator.

See each manager to find out what they have produced.

Clancy

"A manager must deal impartially with both sides of the argument. This is best achieved by examining the rationale behind each point of view and then explaining it to the other side."

Managing Workplace Conflicts

Will

"Facilitation requires three linked actions. First you must establish the position of each party; then you must help each party identify the areas on which they are able to negotiate; and then you must determine how much they will compromise."

Anne

"Mediation needs a solution acceptable to all. So support ways of moving toward a solution, whether you agree with them or not, and when the negotiation starts to falter, suggest alternative compromises."

Clancy, Will, and Anne are interviewed by a writer for the company magazine. They describe some of their successes with mediation.

Anne: My biggest achievement was mediating between two of my team members who were completely deadlocked over the issue of allowing body piercing for the staff. I managed to get them talking about earrings, and they started thinking about visible and invisible piercing. They found an outcome that satisfied both sides.

Clancy: A couple of my staff members shared an office and fought constantly. Finally I asked them who could find a particular office report first. Even though one had a messy desk and one had a tidy desk, neither one could find the report any faster than the other one. My impartial approach helped them to understand that each had his own way of working.

Will: My best intervention as a mediator involved spending lots of time getting the two people to discuss what compromises they were willing to make independently of each other and then bringing them together. We were out of the room with a really good agreement in minutes.

Clancy sums up the approach taken by all of them toward mediation in what becomes the title of the article: "Find the compromises and win!!"

Case Study: Question 1 of 3

Scenario:

For your convenience, the case study is repeated with each question.

You are the area manager at Scattergoods. When you visit the northern outlet, you find yourself acting as a mediator between the office manager, Tad, and his assistant manager, Rachel.

They are unable to agree on the way they should manage the poor performance of one of their staff members.

Answer the following questions, in order, to show how you should mediate between them.

Question:

Rachel says that she thinks you will naturally side with Tad because Tad is her boss. She can't believe that you can mediate effectively at all.

How should you reply to Rachel?

Options:

1. Even though Tad is your boss, I'm going to be impartial. So of course I can mediate without favoritism.

2. Well, I can sort this out easily. One of you is completely wrong on this issue.

3. I am going to listen to you and Tad separately and then explain the positions you take. That is how I will mediate.

4. Of course I can mediate between you and Tad. I'm his boss, so he can't argue with what I say.

5. As a mediator, I have to convince you and Tad that you both have a logical rationale for your arguments.

Answer:

In fact, you need to show impartiality by enabling an appreciation of the content and validity of each side's position.

Option 1: This choice is correct. You should explain to Rachel your intent to be impartial and mediate without favoring Tad. Impartiality is required for effective mediation.

Option 2: This option is incorrect because you are showing partiality before the mediation has even begun. This will not lead to an effective mediation session between Rachel and Tad.

Option 3: This is correct. You should tell Rachel that you will examine the rationale behind each point of view and then explain each to the other side. This process will support impartiality.

Option 4: This is not correct because you are telling Rachel that you will use your authority to pressure Tad into agreeing with your position. This does not demonstrate impartiality, which is what you must do to mediate successfully.

Option 5: This option is correct. It's important to examine the rationale behind the points of view of both Tad and Rachel and then to persuade each person of the validity of the other's argument.

Case Study: Question 2 of 3

Neither Tad nor Rachel have spoken to each other about the problem since the original argument.

How would you facilitate the process of mediation between them?

Options:

1. I'd get them together to talk about something else to reduce tension and anxiety.

2. I'd make sure that I understand each of their positions.

3. I would need to establish an issue they feel they could negotiate on.

4. I would ascertain their willingness to compromise.

5. I'd insist that they stop playing at negotiation and state their intentions and motives.

Answer:

Actually, facilitation will require a good understanding of the negotiable elements of each of their positions. But their willingness to compromise is as important as knowing what they will negotiate about.

Option 1: This option is incorrect because this is not a step that would facilitate the process of mediation. You should take steps to initiate a dialogue about the problem.

Option 2: This option is correct. To start the mediation process between Tad and Rachel, you should first establish each person's position on managing the poor performance of one of their staff members.

Option 3: This is a correct choice. After you have established each person's position, you must then work with Tad and Rachel to identify the areas in which they feel they are able to negotiate.

Option 4: This is correct. After you have established an issue that Tad and Rachel feel they can negotiate on, you must then determine how much they will compromise.

Option 5: This is incorrect. It doesn't sound as though Tad and Rachel have been playing at negotiation; they haven't discussed the problem since they had the argument. This approach is too abrupt and doesn't ease them into the mediation process.

Case Study: Question 3 of 3

Tad believes that the remedy for poor performance is reducing the employee's hours, but he agrees with Rachel that the employee also needs more training. But they don't agree on how to provide time for training. How can you mediate between them?

Options:

1. I'd agree with them about the need for training, even if I think this case requires dismissal as an example to others.

2. I'd suggest to Tad and Rachel that the employee's hours be reduced to allow for more training time.

3. I'd encourage them to formulate a policy on poor performance without reference to this case.

4. I'd get them to decide who was responsible for training and discipline.

Answer:

In fact, to achieve an outcome acceptable to both, you need to encourage any compromises, regardless of your own views, or suggest compromises of your own.

Option 1: This option is correct. Because Rachel and Tad both agree on the need for more training, you should support that solution even if you don't agree with it. The solution should be acceptable to both Tad and Rachel.

Option 2: This choice is correct because you are supporting the idea of increased employee training by suggesting an alternative compromise.

Option 3: This option is incorrect because you're not building on a point of agreement between Tad and Rachel. Rather, you are introducing a new solution that has nothing to do with their positions.

Option 4: This choice is not correct because you are pushing your own agenda rather than supporting a compromise between Tad and Rachel.

Mediation is not a short-term solution. It will take time and effort. But as you have seen, the result will be a compromise that all parties can live with. This means that mediation is a very good way of managing conflict.

Resolving Conflict

Benefits of resolving conflicts

When your kids are fighting, it's natural to separate them. But most parents also want to show them how to get along with each other without quarreling. Managing conflict in the workplace is the same.

Conflict is usually something you have to deal with immediately. Dealing with individual conflicts as they arise is fine, but it can mean that the manager is just putting out one fire after another.

A manager must take a longer-term approach and work on some of the factors that may make conflict less likely to occur. This approach is more apt to truly resolve conflict.

Taking this approach may be difficult when faced with an immediate problem, but you don't have to ignore the present to concentrate on the future. You do need to develop some longer-term strategies that will deal with causes.

By taking a longer-term approach to dealing with both causes and symptoms, you will:
- deal with the existing problem,
- reduce the likelihood of it occurring again,
- create a self-sustaining approach that is general enough to adapt to similar conflicts.

Roxanne can testify to the advantages of taking an approach to managing conflict that deals with the present and the future.

See each time frame to find out how Roxanne describes how this approach to conflict has helped in her organization.

Present

"We were dealing with conflict, and we had to ask why we kept experiencing the same issues. So we analyzed our recurring conflicts."

Future

"Then we could find a way to deal with them. We dealt with the conflict in a way that also stopped it from recurring, and we used that model again and again."

Question

In the fast-moving world of e-commerce, problems have to be solved now. Angel agreed with that but also wanted to take a longer-term approach to the management of conflict in the company. What benefits could he cite to support his proposal?

Options:

1. "A long-term approach will remove the need to analyze each new conflict."

2. "We can concentrate on the future without worrying about the present."

3. "We will still deal immediately with the existing problem."

4. "This approach will be adaptable and transferable enough to deal with similar problems."

5. "By dealing with causes and not just symptoms, we can reduce the likelihood of this problem ever occurring again."

Answer:

Actually, by resolving conflict, you can find current solutions that will cut out future problems and be adaptable to deal with new conflict situations.

Option 1: Incorrect. A long-term approach will not eliminate the need to analyze new conflicts. You may find solutions that will prevent problems or be adaptable to deal with new conflict situations. But to adapt the solutions, you will still have to use analysis.

Option 2: This choice is incorrect. When taking a longer-term approach to dealing with both causes and symptoms, you must also concentrate on the present. Failing to deal with the present could cause more problems in the future.

Option 3: This option is correct. Applying a longer-term conflict management approach will both concentrate on the existing problem and focus on dealing with the root causes to prevent the problem from recurring.

Option 4: This choice is correct. By taking a longer-term approach to dealing with conflict in your company, you will be able to use the model repeatedly to address various problems that may occur.

Option 5: This is correct. When you take a longer-term approach to managing conflict, you will stop it from recurring because you have addressed the underlying causes.

When you resolve conflict, you stop rushing around putting out small fires. So make sure that you are in control. Resolve conflict; don't just react to it.

Goals

What makes for a harmonious organization? You can probably cite many factors, but one factor on most people's list would be common goals.

Now try thinking about it the other way around.

Conflict is often caused by conflicting goals. When parts of the organization are pulling in different directions, then it's really easy for staff members to experience conflict.

Jill has been in exactly that sort of situation, and she found it very difficult and stressful. Here's her story.

I work in customer service. If a package hasn't arrived as promised, I chase it down. Once when I called a warehouse, the manager said that I was preventing his clerks from doing their jobs. I told him I was just trying to do mine. The argument took longer than finding the package.

This is a typical example of conflicting goals. The warehouse manager sees his goal as keeping his staff productive, and Jill temporarily stops his work. So they fight, even though it isn't necessary. They need a common goal.

The most effective way to set goals to resolve conflict is to think of them as being targeted at three levels. This will help to ensure that you have covered all situations.

The three levels are individual, team, and organization. See each piece of advice to find out how to deal with conflict at the three different levels.

Supreme goals supersede individual goals

Organizations are made up of many individuals. If you want to resolve conflict, you must ensure that there is a supreme goal that drives everybody. Individual goals must fit in with this purpose so that potential clashes can be sorted out easily.

Cooperative goals encourage teamwork

Teams show the need for, and the benefit of, cooperative goals. Cooperative goals are goals that require team members to work together. Conflict is resolved because cooperation is essential to achieve these goals. This makes cooperative goals a long-term solution to conflict.

Challenging goals unite everyone in the organization

Even when common goals exist in an organization, they can easily be taken for granted. Then conflict can reappear. One remedy is to develop challenging organizational goals that temporarily supersede the ignored common goal--for example, the goal of surviving an external threat.

So what form do these three types of goals--supreme, cooperative, and challenging--take in the workplace?

Here are some typical examples of these goals and the ways in which they have resolved conflict from various organizations.

Check each type of goal for examples.

Supreme goals

Managing Workplace Conflicts

For Clark and Simon, the memo from David reminding staff members that their ultimate aim was to close the Reno branch by August was timely. Their dispute about needing contract staff ended as they worked on absorbing the Reno people.

Cooperative goals

The finance team members complained about the software team all the time, but when the new audit system forced them to work together to get the systems in place in time, they ended up celebrating together at a party.

Challenging goals

Everyone at Martons knew that repeat customers were the bottom line, but it didn't stop them from fighting every day over new customers. But the CEO's target of a 10 percent increase on repeat business made them stop arguing.

Question

Mac knows that an effective way to resolve long-term conflict in his organization is to ensure that there are common, non-conflicting goals. He also knows that there are different forms of common goals.

Match each form of common goal with one or more appropriate characteristics.

Options:

A. supreme goal
B. cooperative goal
C. challenging goal

Targets:

1. Working together is essential to achieve these goals.
2. This drives every individual.
3. This temporarily supersedes common goals.
4. All individual goals must fit with this purpose.

5. Teams benefit from these goals.
Answer:
In fact, the correct answers identify all the characteristics of the three forms of common goals.

Cooperative goals require team member collaboration. Conflict is resolved because cooperation is essential to achieve these goals.

A supreme goal drives individual actions. To resolve conflict, there must be a supreme goal that drives everyone in an organization toward the same direction.

Challenging goals take precedence over common goals. These goals help resolve conflict by giving an organization a sense of urgency. People must come together to meet a challenging goal.

Individual goals must align with supreme goals so that potential conflicts can be easily resolved.

Teams benefit from cooperative goals because they require team members to work together. Collaborating to meet cooperative goals builds team cohesiveness.

Goal-setting techniques are a valuable part of a manager's armory. They have to be precisely applied in particular ways to resolve conflict.

You will need to consider carefully what you will do to ensure that setting common goals has the maximum impact on resolving conflict.

See each type of goal to learn the best method of conflict resolution.

Supreme goals

Supreme goals are the most typical form of common goals. Their application is therefore straightforward. Ensure that they are clear and understandable and that they really do drive all actions. Use this supremacy to resolve conflict.

Cooperative goals

Cooperative goals resolve conflict when individuals on the team think his or her role as equally valuable in achieving the goal. But this will not resolve future conflict if some individuals receive less credit from the achievement than others.

Challenging goals

Challenging goals have to be exactly that to resolve conflict. They must be sufficiently urgent so that anything that could derail them, like conflict, is eradicated. An effective method is to stress the fallout from missing the goal.

Case Study: Question 1 of 3
Scenario:

For your convenience, the case study is repeated with each question.

You are responsible for the grounds maintenance division at the Caradoc Bowl. This means responsibility for more than 40 staff members in three teams. Conflict among the workforce isn't your biggest problem, but it does create headaches for you, and you want to resolve the conflict as a long-term solution.

Answer the following questions to show how to use common goals to resolve conflict.

Question:

Brett and Daisy argue about the layout for the new garden, which they have been told must be focused on hospitality. Daisy wants it to primarily consist of various flower varieties so that it is innovative. Brett wants it to primarily consist of lawn so that it is easy to maintain. How should you respond to them?

Options:

1. The guiding principle is hospitality. Design a garden that will be best used to entertain our corporate sponsors and their guests.

2. I want you to understand that the motivating force of the garden has to be ecological. When you consider that, the arguments will end.

3. Can't we compromise and have a simple mixture of flowers and grass?

Answer:

In fact, a supreme goal relating to hospitality should be clearly expressed, giving everybody a purpose and helping to resolve conflict.

Option 1: This option is correct because you are reiterating the supreme goal for the garden-- hospitality. Having Brett and Daisy focus on the supreme goal will help stop this conflict and resolve any future conflict between them on this issue.

Option 2: This is incorrect because it doesn't accurately reflect the purpose of the garden. First and foremost, the garden must be focused on hospitality.

Option 3: This choice is not correct. You should not ask Brett and Daisy to strike a compromise without taking into account the primary purpose of the garden-- hospitality.

Case Study: Question 2 of 3

The division seems to have forgotten the mission statement to maintain all the grounds to the highest possible standard. There is a big argument with the parking attendants about who is responsible for the maintenance of the parking area. How should you respond?

Options:

1. Can't you guys remember what our mission statement is? It's "maintain all the grounds."

2. If you don't get your act together soon, the litter in the parking area is going to be taken out of our hands.

3. The stadium owners have told us that unless we solve the litter problem in the parking area, they will send in their own staff at our cost to clean up. Now do you still want to argue?

Answer:

Actually, a challenging goal will usually bring conflicting factions together.

Option 1: This is not correct. Reminding the parking attendants of the common goal will not necessarily resolve the conflict. It won't provide enough motivation for them to change their behavior.

Option 2: This is not correct. You do not stress the urgency of the situation sufficiently to resolve the conflict.

Option 3: This is correct. This emphasizes the urgency of the challenging goal to resolve the conflict between the parking attendants. By stressing the fallout from the external threat, you're forcing the attendants to end their conflict.

Case Study: Question 3 of 3

The inspectors for the annual best-kept grounds awards are on the way, but you have to attend a vital meeting elsewhere. You want Anthony and Jenny, two rival team leaders, to host the inspectors.

How should you tell them this?

Options:

1. I want both of you to host the inspectors at all times so you can each provide immediate answers within your own areas of expertise.

2. Anthony, you take them around and answer any questions. Jenny, that means you only have to organize the lunch for them.

3. Both of you need to make sure that you let them know what your teams have achieved this year.

Answer:

Actually, a genuinely shared cooperative goal giving everybody equal credit will bring conflicting parties to an agreement.

Option 1: This is correct. This is how a cooperative goal will encourage two equally valuable partners to resolve conflict.

Option 2: This choice is not correct. This response doesn't give Jenny equal value in achieving the cooperative goal. Therefore, it is not likely to resolve the conflict.

Option 3: Incorrect. The emphasis on a cooperative goal is undermined by a competitive approach to dealing with the inspectors. This approach stresses the rivalry between Anthony and Jenny and diminishes the likelihood of resolving future conflict.

Goal-setting techniques are used by many organizations as an effective way of managing. When you use them to resolve conflict, you are adding another significant dimension to their value to managers.

Communication

Managing Workplace Conflicts

Have you heard the expression "a war of words"? It's usually used to describe an argument, but it also explains why many arguments happen.

Lester and Jo are having an argument. Can you determine what has gone wrong between them?

Jo: This is stupid. All I need to do is get your permission to present the report, and you want to revise it.

Lester: Of course. I'm not giving you permission If I haven't checked the contents.

Jo: I was told that you simply organized the presentations to the board. Nobody said anything about you checking on the reports.

Lester: Well, that's wrong. In my job description, it clearly states what my role as secretary to the board of directors includes.

Jo: But I've never seen that.

The real problem is ineffective communication causing conflict. If you reconsider the conversation between Jo and Lester, you can find examples of three common communication failings in organizations. These failings reveal the three aspects of communication that managers should be concerned with to improve or reduce the likelihood of unnecessary and destructive conflict occurring in their organization.

See each aspect of communication to learn more.

Language

Part of the problem between Jo and Lester came from their different interpretations of the word "permission." To Jo, it meant arrangements to present the report; to Lester, it meant approval of the contents. Common usage is vital to prevent conflict.

Information

The amount of information each party had was different, so they were bound to clash with one another. Both parties need the same basic information to understand one another. Both assumptions and ignorance lead to conflict.

Channel

Lester mentioned information that was available, but in a way that was inaccessible to Jo. How information is presented--the channel of communication--requires careful consideration to reduce the chance of conflict.

As a manager, you need to make sure that communication in your organization is effective by:
- encouraging the use of unambiguous terms,
- ensuring that sufficient information is available when it is most needed,
- using appropriate and accessible channels to communicate information.

Three companies carefully manage communication to reduce unnecessary conflict situations.

See each company to learn details about how each has organized the communication process.

Carter Phipps

Carter Phipps' workforce is drawn from four professional groups, each with its own technical terms. During orientation, new employees are given a glossary of the most common phrases and terms used. It explains situations in which different usage is likely to cause problems.

Dundee Aggregates

With a history of problems between safety inspectors and site managers, Dundee Aggregates has produced an information brochure detailing the responsibilities for worker safety. It explains the role of the inspectors and how to act in a dispute.

Bod

Bod managers were proud that they used the company intranet to keep the staff informed. However, the dispute with the warehouse workers over vacations made them realize that some blue-collar staff members could not access the intranet easily. They now produce a newsletter for those workers.

Question

The retirement handbook was given to all staff members at orientation, and a Q&A supplement was provided in the year before retirement. It explained all relevant terms clearly and provided a handy calculator for estimating retirement benefits. Which of the qualities of effective communication are evident in this process?

Options:

1. Sufficient information was available to everyone at the times when they most needed it.

2. Giving detailed, personalized information about pension entitlements at orientation was the most appropriate time.

3. The handbook ensured that everybody used common terms.

4. The handbook provided the information in an appropriate manner.

5. A handy calculator for estimating retirement benefits covered both textual and numerical presentation of communication.

Answer:

In fact, if communication is to be effective in resolving conflict, common terms must be used, and everyone should receive sufficient information when it's needed. The channel of communication also needs to be appropriate.

Option 1: This is correct. Giving the retirement handbook to new staff members and the Q&A supplement to those who were about to retire ensured that sufficient information was available when it was most needed.

Option 2: This option is not correct. Providing in-depth, personalized information about pension entitlements at orientation is not the most appropriate time because this information is not needed at that time.

Option 3: This is correct. By explaining all relevant terms clearly, those who created the handbook ensured common language use.

Option 4: This choice is correct. Presenting retirement information in a handbook was an appropriate and accessible channel of communication.

Option 5: This choice is incorrect. Although distributing a calculator helps staff members calculate expected retirement benefits, it does not meet communication goals.

So how do you make communication work for you to resolve conflict in your organization? In essence, you need to control communication so that it works for you and not against you. Stephen Robbins, author of "Organizational Behavior," cites research that suggests that too much, as well as too little, communication can cause conflict. In addition, the wrong forms of communication certainly cause conflict.

Check each aspect to find out how to use communication to resolve conflict.

Language

You need to make sure that language is common to the entire staff. This should involve as much joint training and interchange of ideas among workers as possible. Supplement this with a rigorous ban on jargon and a plain-speaking campaign.

Information

Control the amount of information given to your staff. Too much is as dangerous as too little. So identify the appropriate amount, and avoid the temptation to say more than you have to. Conversely, don't hold back information.

Channel

The channel through which information is passed is vital. Stick to formal systems as much as possible because you can control them, and use a direct method. The more others are involved, the more conflict is likely.

Case Study: Question 1 of 2

Scenario

For your convenience, the case study is repeated with each question.

You are a manager at Techno Lite, and you need to combine two teams. The North and South teams do similar work but in different locations. They have been rivals in the past. You are aware that neither team will welcome this merger and that if handled wrong, it will lead to a major dispute. You must communicate with both of the teams to inform them about the forthcoming merger.

Answer the following questions, in order, to show how to use communication to resolve conflict.

Question

The first meeting you have with the North team begins badly because team members have heard a rumor that they are to be absorbed into the South team. They interpret this as meaning that they will just be assistants.

What should you say to them?

Options:

1. I don't think "absorbed" is the right word. I'd say we're talking more about an anschluss here.

2. You should ignore all of these rumors and only listen to me. I have a formal statement to make.

3. I know that you hate the other team and that you'll never get along with each other, but you have to work together now.

4. "Absorbed" is the wrong word. The teams will be merged, which means that everyone will carry on at

the same level they are currently at.

5. I'm going to speak to your union officials about the merger, and then they will convey the information to you.

Answer:

Actually, to use communication effectively to deal with this conflict, you need to ensure that you control the channel of communication by speaking directly and avoiding ambiguous terms.

Option 1: This is not correct because this comment uses unnecessary jargon that may not be understood by everyone. The use of jargon creates barriers and can lead to conflict.

Option 2: This choice is correct. You need to assert control over the way information is conveyed. A formal statement will be more accurate, will quell rumors, and will minimize conflict.

Option 3: This is incorrect because this statement does not allow you to control information. It offers far too much information and is likely to lead to conflict.

Option 4: Correct. To control language, you need pay close attention to the words you use to convey important information. You should limit jargon as much as possible and define terms when necessary. Jargon creates barriers between people.

Option 5: This choice is incorrect. Allowing the communication to be channeled through union officials may lead to even more conflict.

Case Study: Question 2 of 2

The South team members hear that you have had a meeting with the North team and feel that you are showing favoritism. They want to know what you said to the other team.

What should you say to them?

Options:

1. What I said to them was confidential.

2. I can tell you exactly what I said to them because I am going to say exactly the same things to you.

3. I think to avoid any future problems, we will hold joint meetings so that we all hear the same thing and talk the same language about the merger.

4. I explained how the conflation would work.

5. If you want to know what I said to them, why don't you ask them directly?

Answer:

In fact, you need to control the amount of information you give and try to develop shared experiences to create a common language.

Option 1: This is not correct because this statement demonstrates possible favoritism toward the North team. You should foster shared experiences to create a common language that belongs to both the North and South teams.

Option 2: This is correct. It's important to control the amount of information given to each team. Identify the appropriate amount, and avoid the temptation to say more than you have to.

Option 3: This choice is correct. You need to make sure that language is common to the entire staff. A joint meeting will encourage an interchange of ideas between the teams as well as define a more common language.

Option 4: This option is incorrect because it uses an unnecessary technical term that could create barriers and lead to conflict.

Option 5: This is incorrect because you are relinquishing control of the channel of communication. Conflict is more likely to develop if the South team approaches the North team for the information you gave the North team.

Communication tends to be an instinctive and unconscious activity for most people. But careless communication can so easily lead to conflict. Now you can consciously manage communication in your organization to resolve conflict.

Structures

Picture a car driving down the highway. Gradually the traffic builds, and the car slows until it barely moves. The driver gets more and more frustrated and tries to change lanes. Other drivers won't yield, and the frustration

Managing Workplace Conflicts

escalates. Soon there's a lot of shouting, and then the whole road is full of fighting drivers.

So who's to blame? Well, the drivers, of course, but the situation they were in also caused part of the problem. Too many cars and not enough roads present a structural problem creating conflict.

Many companies have structural problems that cause conflict, and as a manager, you need to know what they are and how to deal with them to reduce the traffic jams in your organization.

Three organizations have typical structural problems that cause conflict among the members of the workplace.

See each company to find out what structural problems they are facing.

Walters Books

Jimmy started work on Monday feeling fine, but by lunch time he was ready to quit. He'd started the report as Mr. Andrews instructed, but then Briony told him to put it aside because she needed him. Somehow, Jimmy was blamed for the big argument that followed.

Donnes

To make an impact at the trade fair, the marketing team at Donnes designed a brilliant new display. The stand area was booked, staff allocated, and the design sent to the builders. Then the finance department decided that the work couldn't be coded to marketing and stopped payment.

Blackley and Prince

When Richie called his best customer, he was told that Don had already taken the order. Richie was in the western sales team, and Don was on the special sales team for the new product line. Both were expected to produce high sales figures this quarter.

As the examples show, there are three key structural elements that are likely to lead to conflict.

They are:
- reporting arrangements and lines of responsibility,
- control of resources,
- the inter-relationships of tasks and functions.

These structural issues are significant because they are the junction points at which workers in the company meet. And like junction points on any road, the traffic has to flow and be managed. The task facing you as a manager is to control and coordinate the interaction of your staff members at these major junction points. So what are the areas of control that managers must understand in order to manage the structural flow of work in their organizations?

Explore each area of control to learn more about managing the structural flow of work.

Interdependence

The key issue here is how some workers, either individually or in teams, can only operate by cooperating and coordinating with others. If someone else controls a key ingredient of their work, then this can be a flash point.

Task uncertainty

The design of the tasks that workers perform affects the likelihood of conflict. Routine tasks cause few problems, but tasks that are uncertain require much more unprogrammed interaction with others. This is a conflict zone.

Time orientation

The time scale by which staff members operate needs examination. Short time scales often clash with longer time scales as workers perform tasks. For example, a research orientation might collide with a production orientation.

The issue of interdependence is quite complicated.

Cary, Richard, and Wendell work in organizations in which workflow problems cause conflict.

Cary: It's a real issue for me. The suppliers have to be paid on time, or the next time I want a discount, I don't stand a chance. Of course, the finance department says that it controls the money, so I have to wait for its systems. If I could just pay up promptly, I'd be fine.

Richard: I always have to check things out with my supervisor, and then I have to discuss it with the design department. I'm constantly stopping, starting, and arguing. Last week, it took most of the day to iron out the different opinions about the packaging because my supervisor told me one thing and the design department told me another.

Wendell: I passed the faulty component along to the technical people immediately. Nothing happened, and when I went to meet them, they said they were still testing it. I said the customer wanted it fixed, not tested, but they said they had to get to the root cause.

Workflow problems are a visible sign of structural problems. In the cases of Cary, Richard, and Wendell, it is possible to link the workflow problem back to its structural cause. This will then give good indicators as to the way to resolve these problems.

See each person to learn more about how to resolve the workflow problems.

Cary

Cary and the finance department need to agree who is in control of that budget. They are interdependent, and this arrangement is causing problems because each side has legitimate ways of operating within its own context. Resource control needs to be structurally managed.

Richard

However, Richard's problem seems more complicated. When his work is so unprogrammed that he can't just do it, then disputes seem inevitable. His work needs to be more routine so that he is only relating to one manager. The tasks need to be restructured.

Wendell

Wendell is facing the problem of time scales. Testing takes longer than fixing. He has an unhappy customer, but the technical group has an interesting problem to solve. Task and support functions are not coordinated to be cooperative.

Interdependence, task uncertainty, and time orientation relate to structural elements that managers need to have under control.

So what should a manager do to resolve structural problems and the way they affect the flow of work in the organization?

Explore each aspect to learn more about the ways to resolve structural problems.

Reporting arrangements

You must actively ensure that a worker has only one boss. Do not leave this problem to sort itself out. Even when two managers are happy to share control, beware of future problems. Formal organization charts are very useful but must be updated.

Control of resources

Avoid conflict by ensuring that those who have responsibility for getting the task done control the necessary resources. Uncertainty about who controls the budget is dangerous. Effective planning and accountability are vital.

Task relationships

Locate support personnel within the physical location of the task when necessary to create good working relationships. Insist on clear reporting arrangements between support staff members and their managers.

Case Study: Question 1 of 2
Scenario:

You are a manager at Treetops Forest Retreat and have become concerned lately by the conflict in your organization.

You ask your assistant manager to prepare a report on the problems and present it to you so you can find ways of resolving them.

Answer the following questions to show how you would resolve the conflict at Treetops.

Question:

Roger is a finance clerk who splits his work between auditing and the purchase ledger. Recently, the chief auditor, ordered Roger to spend all of his time on the forthcoming audit, and Roger failed to complete his tasks on the purchase ledger. When reprimanded by the purchase ledger supervisor, Roger complained to the chief auditor. He is also causing a fuss in the kitchen. Chef Tim has complained that Roger failed to complete the payment of an invoice, so he is now having trouble with that supplier. Roger says that he didn't realize it was so important for that supplier to be paid promptly. What should you do to resolve the conflict?

Options:

1. Identify Roger's boss, and inform everybody of that situation.
2. Make Roger the sole responsibility of Tim.
3. Take budgetary control away from Tim.
4. Send Roger to the kitchen to complete the relevant purchase ledger activities to find out how his support function should operate.

Answer:

In fact, you need to follow the one-worker, one-boss principle to resolve conflict. Putting Roger in the kitchen, if only temporarily, will also help the collaboration between task and support functions.

Option 1: This is correct. You must actively ensure that Roger has only one boss. It is critical to make reporting arrangements simple and clear.

Option 2: This option is not correct because this reporting arrangement is inappropriate. Roger, a finance clerk, should not report to Chef Tim.

Option 3: This choice is incorrect. Taking budgetary control away from Tim won't solve the problem of late payments; it will only transfer the problem to another person.

Option 4: This is a correct choice. If Roger perform his support task in the physical location of the task, he will develop an understanding the task. Roger will also develop a good working relationship with Chef Tim and the kitchen staff.

Case Study: Question 2 of 2

Managing Workplace Conflicts

Tim, the chef, is having trouble with the cleaning staff. He is not happy with the cleanliness of the staff restroom and has ordered the janitors to clean it again. He says he has that right because he controls the cleaning staff's budget. The cleaning staff's boss, the housekeeper, has refused. She says that poor cleaning materials are the problem, and a major argument has ensued. Tim has refused to let the cleaners eat in the staff kitchen.

What should you do to resolve the conflict?

Options:

1. Take the responsibility of the cleaning budget away from Tim and give it to the housekeeper.

2. Put Tim in charge of the cleaners because he controls part of their budget.

3. Make Tim allow the cleaners to eat in the staff kitchen to improve collaboration.

Answer:

Actually, the cause of the conflict is that the cleaning staff lacks control of its own budget. To resolve the problem, give budget control to the housekeeper.

Option 1: This option is correct. To resolve this conflict, you should give the housekeeper direct control of the cleaning staff's budget and resources.

Option 2: This choice is incorrect. The cleaners should report to the housekeeper, who is the supervisor in their task area. Cleaning support personnel should report to their own manager, not a manager of a different area.

Option 3: This option is incorrect. Allowing the cleaners to eat in the staff kitchen doesn't address the underlying problem--that the cleaning staff lacks control of its own budget. Although this may help the situation temporarily, it won't solve the problem.

Sorin Dumitrascu

Structural issues can cause considerable conflict. By using these techniques, you can resolve a large element of conflict in your organization with some simple remedies.

Managing conflict is likely to take about one-third of your time. So whether you want to decrease that time or just make more efficient use of it, the techniques described in this course are a vital guide to the actions you can take.

GLOSSARY

Glossary

E

escalation of arbitration - Escalation of arbitration is when conflict cannot be resolved. The conflict progresses higher and higher up the organization in the search for some sort of resolution.

I

interactionist perspective - This is the view that conflict can be managed to produce positive outcomes.

S

social darwinism - This theory proposes that conflict is the natural human condition and that everyone is dominated by survival instincts.

T

traditional view of conflict - In this view conflict is a negative and destructive force, and to be avoided.

Z

zero sum approach - The zero-sum approach to conflict resolution is one in which the rewards of any negotiated settlement are entirely given to one party.

REFERENCES

References
Understanding Organizations - 1976, Handy, Charles, Penguin
Managing Organizations - 1990, Wilson, D.C. and R.H. Rosenfeld, McGraw Hill
Managers as Negotiators - 1996, Watson, C. and R. Hoffman, Leadership Quarterly
Cultures and Organizations - 1994, Hofstede, Geert, HarperCollins Business
Writers on Organizations - 1964, Pugh, D.S., and D.J. Hickson, Penguin
A Survey of Managerial Interests with Respect to Conflict - 1976, Thomas, K., and W. Schmidt, Academy of Management Journal,

www.ingramcontent.com/pod-product-compliance
Lightning Source LLC
Chambersburg PA
CBHW020901180526
45163CB00007B/2583